D1555218

12·22·76

Too Little But Not Too Late

Too Little But Not Too Late

Federal Aid to Lagging Areas

Sar A. Levitan
Center for Social Policy Studies

Joyce K. Zickler
Center for Social Policy Studies

Lexington Books
D.C. Heath and Company
Lexington, Massachusetts
Toronto

Library of Congress Cataloging in Publication Data

Levitan, Sar A
  Too little but not too late.

  Includes index.
  1. Economic assistance, Domestic—United States. I. Zickler, Joyce K., joint author. II. Title.
HC110.P63L425   338.973   76-12363
ISBN 0-669-00721-8

This Book was prepared under a grant from The Ford Foundation.

Published simultaneously in Canada.

Printed in the United States of America.

International Standard Book Number: 0-669-00721-8

Library of Congress Catalog Card Number: 76-12363

Contents

Preface

The story of federal aid to lagging areas is a tale of attempting to satisfy a Gargantuan appetite with Lilliputian doses. Fifteen years of experience with the Area Redevelopment Administration, the Economic Development Administration, and the Appalachian Regional Commission offer proof positive that it cannot be done. Federal aid to half the United States counties qualifying for economic assistance under the Economic Development Administration accounted in fiscal 1976 for less than one-tenth of one percent of the total federal budget. Assistance to the nineteen million people in Appalachia is scheduled to consume an even smaller proportion of the federal budget.

For every dollar that the federal government is spending this year to promote economic development in lagging areas, more than ten dollars are being spent in these regions to support workers forced into temporary idleness. Clearly, federal policy focuses on providing immediate and direct aid to those in need, and relatively little for preventive measures that would bolster local economies and thereby reduce vast outlays for the unemployed.

Given such minuscule investments to aid depressed areas, their aggregate impact is difficult, if not impossible, to measure. The bulk of these funds is allocated to improving the physical infrastructure of the eligible areas. The Economic Development Administration has concentrated on the construction of public facilities and the mainstay of the Appalachian Regional Commission activities is extensive construction. Instead of indulging in questionable calculations of benefits and costs, this survey summarizes the fifteen years of federal experience in aid to depressed communities and the Appalachian region.

In the first three chapters of the study, the issues underlying the controversies surrounding federal aid to depressed areas are analyzed, and the techniques utilized in designating eligible areas are examined. The next chapter is devoted to a discussion of the role of planning and technical assistance as a tool in economic development. Chapter 5, which is a review of ten years of Appalachian Regional Commission operations, is followed by an analysis of the major EDA activities that have focused on the funding of public works. The declining role of business loans as means of federal assistance to depressed communities is discussed in Chapter 7.

Economic Development Administration and Appalachian Regional Commission officials were generous in sharing data and in offering critical comments on the completed draft. In line with usual practice, the names of these officials are not listed here. I am also indebted to Ralph Widner of The Academy for Contemporary Problems and former executive director of ARC for his review of the Appalachian sections of the volume. Finally, Joyce K. Zickler must be absolved from accountability for the final conclusions of this volume. She left the Center prior to the completion of the study to assume the more glamorous responsibilities of a central banking economist.

The study was prepared under a grant from The Ford Foundation to The George Washington University's Center for Social Policy Studies. In accordance with the Foundation's practice, complete responsibility for the preparation of the volume was left to the authors.

Sar A. Levitan

Center for Social Policy Studies
The George Washington University
March 3, 1976

Too Little But Not Too Late

1 Economic Development Policies and Legislation

The economic history of the United States chronicles the nation's indomitable drive to wealth and power. Blessed with bountiful natural resources and an industrious and skilled labor force, America ascended to affluence in a little more than two centuries. In the eyes of the world, the country's rapid economic, political and social maturation was an enviable and unmatched achievement.

Yet national growth is not a balanced process, and many areas are bypassed by progress while others may experience decline. Natural endowments of resources are unevenly distributed, technological progress brings the rise and fall of industries, and skills become obsolete. Agglomeration economies favor the concentration of growth.

Who is to come to the aid of areas suffering chronic economic depression, and what forms of assistance should be offered?[1] Throughout their economic history Americans developed little taste for planned economics. Capitalism and private initiative were the watchwords for industrial advancement; laissez-faire only began to give way to government intervention in the early twentieth century. The general welfare clause in the Constitution remained largely dormant for a century and a half. Only the Great Depression convinced Americans that the federal government should assume greater responsibility for their social welfare.

The reliance upon the freely fluctuating market mechanism to correct imbalances in economic growth and the belief in the inherent abilities of its work force to adapt to changes in economic conditions meant that until recently the United States made few contributions to regional economic development planning and practices. Ghost towns were assumed to be the price paid for progress and growth that could not be affected by government policy. The most significant exception in the pre-World War II era was the establishment of the Tennessee Valley Authority (TVA) as a federal agency in 1933. The original proposals in 1916 to establish chemical plants at Muscle Shoals and to build the Wilson Dam originated in the nation's World

1

War I munitions needs rather than from any sympathy for economic planning. In the 17 years of debate that followed, the most basic issue was whether to let a private enterprise buy the government's right to the valley's hydroelectric resources.[2] Stimulating the economy of the area was a secondary concern.

Other New Deal economic measures were directed broadly at stimulating employment through a partnership with business and local governments rather than by centralized planning for long-range economic development. The industrial codes and public works projects were designed to put people to work and money in their pockets. At a time when industrial production had been halved and a quarter of the work force was idle, relief programs were inadequate. The economic depression was too pervasive and severe to target aid to the most needy communities. Job creation through the funding of public works construction was a major tool because it provided not only direct employment to the jobless, but also stimulated the demand for building materials.

Depression measures were phased out as the country entered World War II. Growth resulted from the infusion of defense expenditures. Price stabilization and consumer rationing were necessary, and by the end of World War II, America achieved a full employment economy. Fearing a postwar recession, the 1946 Congress declared that the federal government has a continuing responsibility to promote conditions to afford maximum employment opportunities for all willing workers, though specific measures to realize the rhetoric were avoided.

Rapid changes occurred in the U.S. economy during the postwar period. Consumer expenditures were soaring, the industrial pattern was characterized by rapidly growing and declining sectors, agriculture was undergoing a technological revolution, and the geographic dispersion of economic activity was shifting. In the course of his campaign for reelection in 1954, Senator Paul H. Douglas—he was also a leading economist—reviewed the state of the economy and concluded that the rapid expansion of postwar technology was resulting in dislocations for which the adjustment lag might be substantial. He began an uphill struggle to educate decision makers in Washington as well as the public to the need for focusing regional economic development aid on lagging areas characterized by high unemployment, low per capita income, outmigration, downswings in business activity, and deteriorating social capital investments.

Since Douglas first proposed a federal program to aid economically depressed areas, the application of regional development policy in the United States has been debated, researched, experimented with, and evaluated. Economic development programs have never won acceptance as a tool of economic policy and have remained a half-hearted effort—a cross between welfare and economic stimulation—to help lagging areas. The programs' funding has been meager and the controversy over their value and success, interminable. The emerging grassroots support was effective in saving the programs when President Nixon sought their demise, but lacked clout or resources to work for the expansion of federal aid to depressed areas. The Council for Urban Economic Development, a professional organization of economic developers, also helped the cause of federal aid for depressed areas. Consisting of some 300 consultants, public officials, and a sprinkling of academics, the organization is prohibited from lobbying, but its members are not denied the right to engage in missionary and educational work.

The Issues

The Role of the Federal Government

The view persists that over the long run competitive forces in the economy, if allowed to operate unhindered, will result in an optimum level and desired distribution of economic activity. To those holding that belief, depressed areas are only a short-run phenomenon or an inevitable natural development, and people and industries stranded in lagging regions must bite the bullet while competitive market forces seek a new equilibrium. In the long run, according to this view, the problems of depressed areas will be resolved. Government action, they argue, is unnecessary and, in fact, might cause costly disruptions in the free enterprise system and eventually be counterproductive by misallocating and wasting resources. Although the outlook may appear gloomy for declining areas, if the government pursues stimulative aggregate demand policies, lagging areas will be pulled up as the national economy grows. The persistence of labor surplus areas during the near full-employment years of the 1960s, however, is evidence that necessary adjustments may take decades, if they ever materialize.

On the other side are those who believe that the much-heralded models of competition fail to recognize the immobility of workers and capital resources, misallocation of investment, and failure to achieve the promises of scale economies. As in other sectors of American economic and social life in the postwar period, government involvement in the private as well as the public economies of poor regions has grown. Proponents argue that depressed areas lack the resources to catch up with national growth and that gains may be made in encouraging a more desirable distribution of people and industry than dependence on market forces will bring.

The issue of government intervention versus free markets became transformed into clashes between fiscal liberals and conservatives in the political arena, the former winning enough battles to keep aid to depressed areas alive, and the latter successful in keeping appropriations low.

The Promise of Federal Aid

Proponents of economic development assistance to lagging and depressed areas argue that balanced and more even geographic growth is essential. The absence of such a policy, they suggest, has resulted in unfettered metropolitan growth accompanied by socially costly pollution, congestion, crime, and other urban ills. The social benefits of discouraging outmigration from declining rural areas and the development of industry and community facilities in rural areas will bring a net gain in social welfare to the country.

There are other potential benefits of aid to depressed regions. Increased economic activity can create jobs for idle or underutilized workers. Earned income may be expected to replace transfer payments; tax receipts may improve local government finances. Capital for further expansion may flow into local lending institutions.

Some industries could reduce their costs by locating in small towns and rural settings, as occurred with the relocation of northern textile mills in low-wage southern areas. Underdeveloped areas, however, would prefer to attract industry on the basis of other inducements, such as improved community facilities and skilled workers, which require considerable investments before business will find the areas attractive. Also, short-term assistance to utilize unemployed human and natural resources might help depressed areas back on the road to competition for private business activity. This argument resembles that for protection of infant industry from foreign competition.

Means and Costs

The costs of attempting to achieve these benefits depend on the tools chosen to do the job. The programs made available over the past 15 years have fallen into three main categories: grants and loans for public facilities, loans to private businesses, and a variety of technical assistance, research, and planning support. Accelerated tax amortization and other tax privileges for private enterprise have been used sparingly during World Wars I and II and the Korean Conflict to stimulate production and to encourage favored industrial and business activity. The Ford administration, however, has proposed reviving the use of such assistance in high unemployment areas. Defense Manpower Policy No. 4, which has been in effect since 1953, allows firms in depressed areas to receive preference in the award of government contracts if they bid below or equal to the average of all bids received.

The above tools do not exhaust the list of options for assistance to depressed areas. Various European countries have tried low interest regional development funds and investment grants to influence the location of industry.[3] Since the 1930s the United Kingdom has attempted to encourage dispersion of industry from the London-Birmingham areas. The policy includes inducements for location in redevelopment areas in the form of cash grants and restraints to prevent location in congested regions by requiring prior permits. France, too, encourages growth away from Paris with grants, indemnities, accelerated depreciation allowances, relocation assistance, and other tax breaks. Location in Paris is taxed. The French also have favored a growth center policy by offering preference in the allocation of public works and the funding of cultural amenities in depressed areas with growth potential.

In the United States opponents have equated proposals involving industrial relocation with industrial piracy; special assistance for depressed areas has not been popular. Industrial licensing has not been acceptable, although zoning laws frequently determine the location of economic activity in urban areas. Relocating workers has failed to gain support as well. Efforts contributing more indirectly than directly to attracting industry have been preferred, namely, grants or subsidies for public facilities, industrial parks, water and sewer lines, and highways.

Who Is Really Helped?

The tools must be judged on their abilities to help needy people as well as needy places. Some wellworn tools, such as the building of industrial sites and loans to induce the location of new or expansion of established business, can be expected to stimulate economic activity and, on the basis of jobs and income created, to improve an area's economic health. But if the new opportunities fail to impact the lives of the chronically unemployed or underemployed residents of the area, perhaps because the jobs created are taken by new migrants or demand skills that area residents lack, the program has fallen short of its goal.

Moving jobs to labor surplus areas aids the unemployed only if they are capable of filling the newly-created openings. Some idle workers may require basic education, training, and health programs to prepare them to take advantage of expanding employment opportunities. Antidiscrimination efforts must be undertaken to open doors for the unemployed once they qualify to fill the jobs. If jobs are not created for them, the needy would be served better by assistance in migrating to growing areas. Although the logic of this approach may seem oversimplified, it bears repeating in light of the failure of U.S. policy makers to organize efforts based on a recognition of the interdependence of human resources and economic development programs.

This is not to suggest that the two strategies are mutually exclusive. Poverty and dependence are not confined to lagging regions; help should be available to the disadvantaged wherever they reside. But comprehensive aid programs must be aimed at those specific areas where job deficits are chronic and are accompanied by structural economic dislocations. Unless training and economic development efforts are coordinated, industrial subsidies could result in the immigration of skilled workers from other areas, creating even greater inequality in income distribution and pressuring local governments to expand public services while their tax base deteriorates.

Even the most ardent advocates of government intervention in depressed economies do not claim that economic development programs could cure the ills of all depressed areas. Realistically, not all lagging areas have economic potential. Welfare programs to relieve deprivation or skill training and relocation assistance for the employable are appropriate ways to help persons stranded in areas so depressed that they cannot be expected to respond to economic development aid. The challenge to policy makers is to target aid to the most needy areas and, at the same time, make the most cost-effective investments of tax dollars.

Federal Aid to Depressed Areas

During the past two decades the debate on aid to depressed areas centered on the Area Redevelopment Act of 1961, its successor, the Public Works and Economic Development Act of 1965, and the Appalachian Regional Development Act of 1965. In each case, economic policy was tempered with political considerations. The confrontation of politics and economics has been crucial in shaping U.S. economic development programs.

The Area Redevelopment Act

The Area Redevelopment Act of 1961 marked the first time in U.S. history that a program of development tools was added to the arsenal of federal economic policies. During the protracted six-year debate preceding the bill's passage, the practicability of translating economic intentions into a legislative mandate was discussed at length. Although less than $400 million in appropriations was at stake, the Area Redevelopment Act deliberations drew many of the lines on the appropriate federal role in regional development policy that have extended into the current consideration of the future of economic adjustment legislation.[4]

Senator Paul H. Douglas first conceived a program of public works, long-term business credit, technical assistance, and extension of unemployment benefits to jobless workers if they undertook a retraining course. The Eisenhower administration opposed federal assistance to depressed areas, relying upon expansionary national policy to solve the job deficits of lagging areas. When pressures for aid mounted, the Eisenhower administration proposed a revolving business loan program for depressed areas. As the two views evolved, the debate centered on whether the most effective way to aid lagging areas or regions was with aggregate demand or structural economic policies.

The Douglas proposal, spelled out in a bill which he first introduced in 1955, provided for revolving funds for public facilities as well as private businesses, a training program for the unemployed, and accelerated tax amortization privileges for businesses locating or expanding in depressed areas, but the bill stated no specific requirements. Although his original intention was to aid chronically depressed industrial areas, the need for broad political support in Congress led to the addition of a special provision for business loans to firms in low-income rural areas, and the ante for public facilities was raised to allow for rural eligibility. Even at these early stages, it was obvious that the notion of targeting aid to the most depressed areas had to be compromised in the face of political pressures to attract the widest support for the program.

Perhaps more significant in the battle to gain support for aid to depressed areas, both in Congress and with the public, were the ups and downs of the business cycle between 1955 and 1961. The Senate first approved depressed area legislation in 1956, but since the economy was expanding and there were few labor surplus areas, the Eisenhower administration felt secure in its opposition, which killed the bill in the House. By the 1958 congressional elections, the economy was in a recession. The Douglas bill was revived and passed both houses only to be vetoed by President Eisenhower. Unemployment, then, became a major campaign issue, and in many areas potentially eligible for aid Democrats replaced Republicans in Congress. As a result, support for depressed area legislation was bolstered at the beginning of the 1959 session. But congressional action was delayed as support dwindled during the economic recovery, and the administration blamed overspending by the Democratic Congress for the mounting budget deficit. When Congress passed the Douglas depressed area bill again in 1960, President Eisenhower used the veto once more.

The next national economic slump coincided with a presidential election, and John F. Kennedy had won a crucial primary victory in West Virginia where he campaigned on the depressed area theme. The

Douglas bill received top priority in the Kennedy administration, and the president signed the Area Redevelopment Act on May 1, 1961. Owing to the protracted legislative battle, the legislation's original theoretical base as a structural tool to target aid to areas of persistent economic malaise was ignored, and the Area Redevelopment Act became associated with curing persistent unemployment and low income as well as temporary job deficits due to cyclical downswings. Even more inauspicious for the Area Redevelopment Act, the program was initiated during an economic recession—precisely the environment when efforts to alleviate structural problems have the least impact.

Except for the expansion of target areas and the deletion of rapid tax amortization, the provisions of the 1961 law varied little from the original Douglas proposal. Funds were authorized for business loans, public facilities grants and loans, training unemployed workers, and technical assistance grants to encourage economic planning, feasibility studies, and research. On the assumption that the lack of venture capital is a major stumbling block to attract business to depressed areas, the most sizable appropriations were for loans. To prepare workers to qualify for the anticipated new jobs that the loans and public works would attract, the Act provided for the retraining of workers and for the payment of stipends to workers undergoing training. The meager funds appropriated were hardly adequate for the broad assistance menu and by 1965 the Area Redevelopment Act approved a total of $323.3 million, divided as follows:

405 Industrial and commercial loans	$176.1 million
157 Public facilities grants and loans	$104.1 million
486 Technical assistance projects	$ 16.1 million
1,416 Training courses	$ 25.6 million
44 Research projects	$ 1.4 million

The long legislative debate had promoted an awareness of the problems faced by depressed areas and had settled, at least temporarily, several issues in economic development. The Area Redevelopment Act established federal responsibility to intercede in areas subject to economic dislocations and laid to rest the spurious charge equating federal aid with interference in private business decisions and undercutting of the free enterprise system. The worries of some congressmen that the aid would encourage businesses to leave their districts and relocate in competing areas were soothed by disqualifying runaway shops from Area Redevelopment Act assistance.

Passage of the Area Redevelopment Act did not settle many other issues in economic development, such as whether to concentrate aid on people or places. The Act recognized the need to combine investments in training with investments in plant and equipment, but the vocational training efforts were timid by comparison with assistance to business and were soon overshadowed by the Manpower Development and Training Act of 1962, which provided similar assistance to unemployed persons regardless of the unemployment level in their areas of residence. Defense Manpower Policy No. 4, initiated in 1953 to offer labor surplus areas preference in federal procurement, supplemented the Area Redevelopment Act's provision for the unemployed. Relocation assistance and labor mobility projects for depressed areas remained live issues. The Trade Expansion Act of 1962 included the former, and the Labor Department experimented half-heartedly with the latter. Another controversy centered on the proper mix of tools, including the relative merits of loans and grants and the appropriate role of private versus public projects.

The Area Redevelopment Act economic development tool kit was to apply to all areas designated as needy, no matter what the roots of the distress. It was obvious from the outset that the Area Redevelopment Administration would have a difficult time stretching its funds to cover all the eligible areas. How to draw geographical boundaries and to set standards for eligibility became a continuing debate. The Act called for counties to be the basic unit of eligibility, and money was to flow directly into local hands from the federal spigot. The Area Redevelopment Act depended on low income and unemployment to measure need for much the same reason that other social programs did—the ready availability of data—despite the fact that such sweeping standards did not distinguish between structural and cyclical problems or among the different roots of economic dislocations.

Accelerated Public Works (APW)

With unemployment rising during the first half of 1961 and remaining sticky in its decline, the Kennedy administration favored a more vigorous federal attack on "excess" unemployment above the 4 percent interim acceptable level. Besides a tax cut, President John F. Kennedy favored a new and much larger program of public works grants even before the Area Redevelopment Administration tooled up to put into operation the 1961 Act.[5]

Kennedy's request for a permanent standby authority to spend up to $2 billion on capital improvement met stiff opposition in Congress. Conservative Republicans and southern Democrats refused to make a "political slush fund" available at the President's discretion, not to mention their opposition to the pump-priming strategy. In September 1962 Congress authorized the expenditure of $900 million for accelerated public works projects, but rejected the proposed standby authority.[6]

Only $400 million was appropriated for fiscal 1963, and when Kennedy requested the remainder in supplemental appropriations, the specter of a slush fund was revived. Nonetheless, Congress appropriated an additional $484 million, including $30 million for fiscal 1964 and $4 million for 1965. Although the House Public Works Committee tried to up the ante late in 1963, the administration had dropped its support for renewal of the program in favor of a tax cut.

Regional development issues played only a minor role in the Accelerated Public Works debate. Unemployment was the overriding concern; average national unemployment stood at 5.8 percent, and numerous areas with 6 percent or more unemployment qualified for assistance. Area eligibility was hardly an issue, and controversy centered on legislating presidential authority to distribute money without specific prior congressional approval. The Act called for projects that would provide "immediate useful work for unemployed and underemployed." Projects were limited to those that could be initiated and completed in a reasonable time, and half the allocated funds were to be expended in a year after projects were approved and funds allocated. Despite their short run nature, the Area Redevelopment Administration was called on to coordinate the new program. Those who favored the continuation of the program noted that it was not only intended to have a countercyclical effect, but also to offer depressed areas a much needed opportunity to improve their infrastructure. The hope was that, in the long run, the construction of water, sewage, and other community facilities would encourage business growth and ward off outmigration.

Appalachian Regional Development Act

The next economic development undertaking focused on an area that had become synonymous with structural regional economic dislocations. The economic and social isolation of the Appalachian region, the waste of its forests, and the ravages of its coal-bearing mountains have attracted attention since the days of Thomas Jefferson. The Great Depression brought New Deal welfare and public works programs to the area.[7] Most New Deal measures were concerned with job creation and did not address themselves to the region's longer-run needs. The major exception was the establishment of the Tennessee Valley Authority, which not only advanced the development of some sections of the southern Appalachian region, but also promoted intergovernmental cooperation. Despite a brief reprieve during World War II when the demand for coal increased, the economy of Appalachia had failed to adjust to continued postwar changes in U.S. economic structure, and its economic development had continued to lag.

Appalachia benefited from Area Redevelopment Act and Accelerated Public Works funds; almost a third of ARA dollars and a fourth of APW funds were expended on projects in the region. But even before these programs were enacted, a movement for a separate regional program was getting under way. Eastern Kentucky businessmen formed a development council in 1956, and after a severe flood swept through the area in January of the following year, the state authorized a permanent regional planning council.[8] In 1959, at hearings before the Senate Special Committee on Unemployment Problems, the Kentucky group presented its case for federal support of a regional planning body allying all the states along the Appalachian chain. Senator John Sherman Cooper of Kentucky was the lone supporter of a broad Appalachian development program.

The next organizational step was taken in 1960 by Governor J. Millard Tawes of Maryland who convened two meetings of the region's nine governors. Undecided on the details of a proposal for a regional commission, the governors acceded to the White House creation of a liaison staff within ARA to work with them to apply ARA dollars to Appalachia.

Another flood disaster in March 1963 revived the regional commission proposal. This time Kennedy established the President's Appalachian Regional Commission (PARC) representing 14 federal agen cies and the nine states. For a year PARC studied the needs of the region and extracted proposals from practically all federal agencies on how they could expand their current programs to give special attention to Appalachia's problems. The Commission defined development more broadly than just as economic stimulation. The final report called for highway, human resources, natural and water resources programs, as well as the establishment of a regional development commission. The proposed programs carried an immediate price tag of over $220 million.[9]

The design of an agency to administer the Appalachian program was controversial. A 1964 bill failed in the House of Representatives because it called for the creation of a TVA-like public corporation with component local development corporations. As a result, the 1965 bill called for a more acceptable federal/state commission to oversee Appalachian aid. President Lyndon Johnson was opposed to the idea of a regional development commission, preferring a federally-controlled program. Nevertheless, he was committed to fight a war on poverty, and Appalachia had to be an important theater of operations.[10] The Democratic landslide in November 1964 assured eventual passage of the Appalachian Regional Development Act, and in March 1965 President Johnson signed it as another plank in the Great Society structure.

No one could deny that the economic problems of Appalachia had persisted regardless of the state of the national economy, and that the Great Society was morally obligated to send aid. What was unique in the Appalachian legislation was the special federal/state partnership provided to coordinate the flow of federal dollars into the region. Title I created the Appalachian Regional Commission composed of a presidentially appointed federal member and representatives of each of the region's governors. The Commission was given broad authority to develop plans and programs, encourage private investment, conduct research, make recommendations to the President and the governors on Appalachian aid, promote interstate cooperation, and coordinate Appalachian programs.

The Act authorized $840 million to be spent over six years for highways. Approximately $245 million was to be expended over a two-year period for health, conservation, vocational education, and other human resources and development efforts. Over half of these funds supplemented existing programs.

Intergovernmental relations aside, the Appalachian program varied in several other respects from previous economic development programs. Industrial loans and subsidies intentionally were not included, and the federal share of public works funds were limited largely to highway construction (Figure 1-1). Appalachia, it was presumed, would continue to receive industrialization and public works monies from ARA or its successor. The goal of the Appalachian Regional Development Act was to provide aid to make up for some of the other glaring deficiencies in the region—lack of access

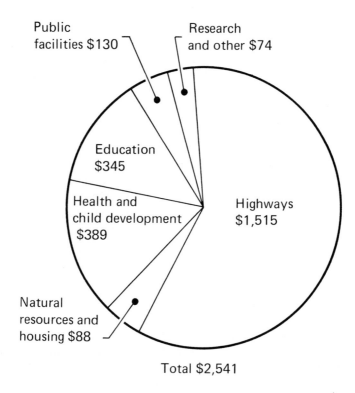

Total $2,541

Note: Because a variety of sources were utilized, data in this figure and elsewhere do not necessarily coincide.

Source: *1975 Annual Report of the Appalachian Regional Commission* (Washington: The Commission, 1976), adjusted from table 6.

Figure 1-1. Appalachian Regional Commission Appropriations, 1966-1975 (Millions).

routes, health facilities, and vocational training sites—as well as to restore the ravaged land. It embodied a recognition of the wide-ranging deprivation attendant in a depressed area. The Appalachian Act must be viewed in conjunction with the other Great Society efforts. Initially, at least, prime responsibility for the development of human resources and welfare programs was placed under the antipoverty agencies, while the Appalachian Regional Commission was to focus on bolstering the physical infrastructure of the region.

ARA Under Fire

By 1965 sentiment had built among friends and foes alike to restructure ARA's economic development programs of the previous four years. Disappointment had begun to surface almost immediately following the Area Redevelopment Act's implementation. Though popular, Accelerated Public Works programs had expired. Further, President Johnson had promised to create more regional commissions like the Appalachian to join the march toward the Great Society.

Dissatisfaction with the Area Redevelopment Administration's performance was the hottest issue. Burdened with inefficient procedures that required the parent agency to distribute applications to other federal agencies for approval, the Area Redevelopment Administration was able to disburse only a portion of its funds in its first two years. This was particularly detrimental to the agency's public facilities grants program, which had exhausted its funds by the end of fiscal 1963 largely because Congress refused to reappropriate the funds that were not used during the first year of operation. Loans for public facilities were unattractive, on one hand, because most communities could obtain loans on which the interest was tax exempt in the open market and, on the other, because the Accelerated Public Works Act injected five times the money available under the Area Redevelopment Act into grants covering up to 50 percent of public works projects.

Once the Area Redevelopment Administration began distributing funds, the agency was accused of unwise investments and favoritism. Since business loans were confined by law to companies unable to obtain conventional loans, only more risky or marginal firms could apply. Established businesses opposed the agency's financing of competitors and conventional lenders protested its intrusion into the loan market charging less than going rates of interest. Other problems included the weakness of local planning capability and the scarcity of local funds to meet the requirement that areas contribute 10 percent of agency-backed projects. Finally, compounding all these difficulties was the downturn in the economy during 1961 and the persistence of high unemployment. Stimulating new business activity seemed especially fruitless when economic contraction had caused a nation-wide underutilization of capacity.

Congress was no help; on the contrary, it added to the Area Redevelopment Administration's woes by expanding eligibility, leaving the agency little choice but to spread its limited funds too thinly. The eligibility criteria for accelerated public works were even looser. Still the lawmakers expected, or at least said so in their speeches back home, a noticeable return in their individual districts for their support of the Area Redevelopment Act. Such visible results were unrealistic in light of the Area Redevelopment Administration's meager resources, and agency spokesmen only complicated matters by issuing inflated evaluations of its success.

The Public Works and Economic
Development Act of 1965

Beset by administrative problems, the economic development program needed a face-lifting and a broader based appeal to regain congressional support. The Johnson administration stressed the positive side of economic development—community facilities built and new industries located—and promised to improve the law through long-range planning, the concentration of aid in areas with growth potential, and the establishment of more regional commissions (Figure 1-2).

Like the Appalachian bill, the Public Works and Economic Development Act of 1965 faced no great difficulties in Congress after the Democratic landslide of the fall. Following a two-month extension of the Area Redevelopment Act to keep from breaking stride, the new five-year authority for economic development programs became law on August 26, 1965.

The law provided for public works and development facilities grants—for projects similar to those under the accelerated public works program of 1962—and authorized an annual expenditure of

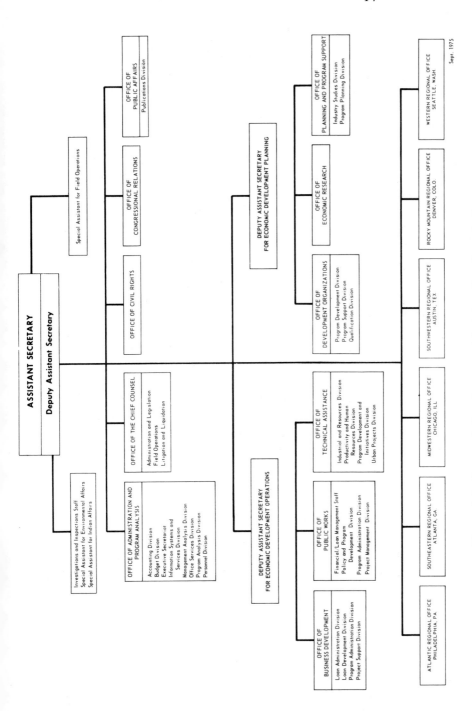

Figure 1-2. Economic Development Administration Organization.

$500 million for four years. Congress downgraded reliance upon loans by authorizing $170 million annually for public and for private business development efforts. Another $25 million of annual appropriations was authorized for technical assistance to areas needing help in evaluating their economic potential.

In response to criticism of the Area Redevelopment Administration's overextension and in an effort to make economic development dollars more cost-effective, Congress mandated the identification of growth centers—"economic development centers"—of less than 250,000 people, provided the aid would have beneficial spillover effects on depressed areas. Fifty million dollars could be spent each year in these areas in grants, loans, or loan guarantees. The goal was to encourage labor market or larger area economic planning. These areas were to be part of multicounty economic development districts combining at least two eligible depressed areas with a growth center to prepare joint economic development plans.

Representatives of the Great Lakes, Ozarks, and New England suggested that their areas, too, were worthy targets of the regional development approach. Their views were incorporated in the provision that called for the establishment of regional commissions, but failed to specify adequate funds for their support. Federal financial assistance was limited to $15 million annually to be used for technical assistance and administrative costs to establish multistate agencies for planning economic development programs.

Apart from the inclusion of special growth center funds and the new planning agencies, EDA marked little change in U.S. economic development rationale. Job training had been separated from the rest of ARA's original development tools and turned over to the Departments of Labor and Health, Education, and Welfare. This action did not reflect a change in policy, but rather a congressional affirmation of practice that evolved with the implementation of federally-funded training programs since 1962. The other tools—public works projects, business grants and loans, and technical assistance—were left in the hands of the Department of Commerce. No new vehicles were added. Instead, the motivation behind the legislation was to consolidate the earlier efforts and improve program performance, not to alter the basic content of the programs. Public works had gained popularity in Congress, and their appropriations far outweighed other portions of the law, accounting for 73 percent of Economic Development Act obligations during its first decade (Figure 1-3). Business loans, which

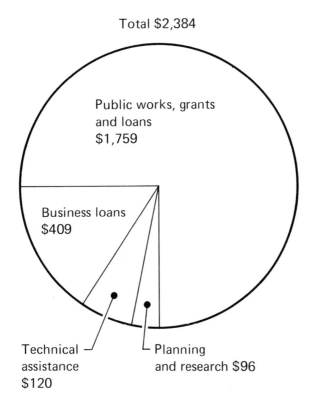

Total $2,384

Public works, grants
and loans
$1,759

Business loans
$409

Technical
assistance
$120

Planning
and research $96

Source: U.S. Department of Commerce, Economic Development Administration, *1975 Annual Report* (Washington: Government Printing Office, 1975), in press.

Figure 1-3. Economic Development Act Obligations, 1966-1975 (Millions).

were the cornerstone of the Area Redevelopment Act, declined in importance and constituted only a fifth of Economic Development Act obligations compared with more than half of Area Redevelopment Act outlays.

Although short-lived, experiences under the Area Redevelopment Act and the Accelerated Public Works Act left their mark. The premise that federal aid was needed had become accepted; the camel's nose was in the tent, but he remained a pretty small camel. The greater reliance on public works instead of loans was a testament to their political popularity rather than to any evidence of the long-run impact in attracting jobs to economically depressed areas. Finally, giving aid to needy areas was favored as long as the need criteria were left loose, and every area with a legitimate claim could apply.

Recent Issues in Economic Development Policies and Legislation

Countercyclical Public Works

During the Great Society years, economic development programs aroused little controversy. The Nixon administration, however, opposed the continuation of categorical economic development programs and proposed that they be absorbed under a broader revenue-sharing program. The proposal failed to gain support in a Congress more concerned with measures to combat unemployment than with revamping the administration of federal programs. The four-year extension of the Economic Development Act that emerged from Capitol Hill in 1970 included the authorization of a $2 billion accelerated public works program. The President vetoed the bill, calling it inflationary and an inefficient way to create jobs, but acceded to a later bill that merely set aside up to a quarter of the Economic Development Act's public works money for a Public Works Impact Program (PWIP) for projects that could be completed quickly and would create jobs in high unemployment areas.

Congress persisted in its plans to incorporate countercyclical and overall job creation measures in Economic Development Act programs. President Nixon vetoed a 1972 bill providing $3 billion in added authorizations and new funds for public works jobs.

Congress yielded to Ford administration pressure when the Act was extended in 1974 and reduced the minimum PWIP allocation to 10 percent of public works funds. But, faced with a deepening recession, Congress passed the Emergency Jobs and Unemployment Assistance Act. The $5.93 billion appropriations included $500 million for the Job Opportunities Program attached as Title X to the Economic Development Act. Since the bulk of the funds were for public service jobs, summer youth programs, and extensions of unemployment insurance, President Ford approved the bill despite his opposition to the public works provision. Congress rejected the President's attempt to rescind funds for the Job Opportunities

Program, and continued to propose even larger programs for 1976. Countercyclical public works likely will remain a source of conflict in future considerations of economic development assistance—the popularity of public works assuring broad support for the expansion of federal job creation activities.

Economic Adjustment Assistance

Although an extension of the Economic Development Act was signed in 1973, the administration sought to abolish the agency by requesting no funds for its programs. At the same time, however, the 1973 bill called on the President to reexamine economic development programs and to report findings to Congress. The debate between the Nixon administration and Congress over the fate of the Economic Development Administration resulted in the addition of another new title to the law in 1974.

The administration's new plan—named after Senator Henry L. Bellmon of Oklahoma who proposed the report—was prepared by the Office of Management and Budget and reflected the ideology of the agency.[11] It proposed a modest revenue-sharing program of grants to states that would redistribute aid to substate areas for public facilities, business loans and guarantees, planning, research and technical assistance.

Congress rejected the revenue sharing, but the administration's proposal was adopted in a modified form under a new Title IX that allows the Economic Development Administration to provide funds in areas threatened by unemployment due to plant and military closings or other dislocations. In addition to loans, and guarantees, and technical assistance, funds could be used for training, relocation, mortgage assistance, and unemployment compensation. Unlike under the administration's original plan, local governments can apply as well as states.

A second economic adjustment program administered by the Economic Development Administration is part of the Trade Act of 1974. Business loans and working capital guarantees are available to firms in which unemployment or a substantial decrease in sales is threatened because of foreign competition caused by U.S. trade agreements. Both programs are supposed to test whether preventive adjustment programs can forestall economic dislocations hopefully before unemployment and income loss become severe. The efforts are relatively small, however, and it is doubtful whether the resources allocated can effectively test the efficacy of early economic warning signals. Title IX was funded at $38.8 million for fiscal 1975 and $62 million for 1976; $15 million was available in 1976 under the Trade Act. Nevertheless, the Economic Development Administration repeatedly has been criticized as a program that is able only to react, not act, to help depressed areas. Perhaps an ounce of prevention is a good start.

A Future for Economic Development Programs

Clearly, specially designed economic development programs are a small part of an overall economic policy. Their impact on depressed economies is difficult to measure or to assess, since economic aid to depressed areas is a fraction of total federal help to these areas. Congressional committee structure, competing special interests, and the failure of interagency coordination have contributed to create fragmented programs with related purposes. A single economic development policy for the country appears improbable.

One criticism of current economic development programs is their inability to treat illnesses until after they occur. Critics also point out that even if early warning efforts to alleviate economic dislocations were designed, the minuscule size of the programs would render economic aid to depressed areas ineffective. The meager sums available under EDA's and ARC's economic development programs—under $500 million annually—pale in comparison to total federal public works construction expenditures, which now total approximately $13 billion annually, or to aid to the unemployed, which in 1975 amounted to nearly $20 billion.

The dissatisfaction with the impact of current economic development efforts has resulted in several attempts to define more comprehensively a national growth policy and to consolidate as many development programs as possible under a single mandate. The House Banking and Currency Committee, whose interests traditionally focused on housing and urban problems, has indicated interest in a national growth policy. The House Public Works Committee, which oversees the Economic Development Act and the Appalachian program is examining the elements of a national public works investment policy. At the same time Congress has created new economic development responsibilities in programs authorized by the Consolidated Farm and Rural Development Act of 1972, bringing the Agriculture Committees in Congress and the Department of Agriculture into the economic development arena.

Other charges against the current economic development programs reflect the distaste for and inefficiency of project-by-project decision making at the federal level and the lack of multilevel government and private involvement. The debate persists on what institutions and levels of government are most appropriate to administer economic development programs. The Nixon administration advanced several proposals to place more control over funds in the hands of state and local officials. Opponents raised serious questions about the capabilities of state and local decision makers, the capabilities of intergovernmental organizations, and the proper role for the federal government in identifying areas of need and monitoring the investments.

The mix of economic development programs has again surfaced in several policy issues. First, should the emphasis on public works investments continue? Should job creation be the major consideration or is there a role for social development and human resources programs in economic development? Is there a continuing role for antirecessionary programs meant to alleviate short-run economic ills in a program whose larger mandate is to mitigate the impact of structural economic charges?

A decade of EDA and ARC offered a timely occasion for a review of U.S. economic development efforts. The time was ripe to reexamine the rationale for aid to depressed areas, to identify what constitutes need, to evaluate the tools available to help, and to analyze whether federal/state/local partnership of public and private interests could be organized better to put economic development programs to work. Ambitious observers suggest that such a review be supplemented with a study of a national policy of balanced urban and rural growth to promote better distribution of population. Regrettably, the economic slump in the mid-1970s turned attention to more pressing and pervasive problems facing the American economy. In this climate, concern for lagging communities had to take a back seat, even if their problems were aggravated by the deepest economic recession in more than three decades.

2

People, Places, and Economic Lag

Growth and Decline in the United States

Growth patterns in the United States have varied significantly by region since World War II, and with them the types of economic adversity. Many growing areas of the West face unemployment associated with inmigration and shifts in demand for defense industry output. In New England reduced demand for leather goods, textiles, and shoes has struck a hard blow at the manufacturing base. While the North Central region was the least affected by unemployment over the past twenty-five years, its upper reaches around the Great Lakes have been in an economic decline as its forests and mineral resources were depleted. The South included the most depressed segments of the Appalachian region, the Black Belt, and the Mississippi Delta. Chronic unemployment and underemployment abound in all these areas, largely among blacks in rural agricultural and often isolated communities.

Two special cases of economic need—the Indians on reservations and minorities in urban ghettos—are scattered throughout the nation. Perhaps the most debilitating combination of economic and social problems—few natural resources, an unskilled labor force, poverty, ill-health, crime and chronic job deficits—is found on the nation's Indian reservations. Although the economies of the reservations and those of the regions where they are located are unrelated, a significant proportion of the needy population in the Southwest resides on reservations. Urban ghettos account for even more sizable concentrations of poverty, unemployment, underemployment, and low earnings, even when employment is available. These concentrations of need contrast with the scattered target populations of the rural South or Upper Great Lakes.

The variety and distribution of economic distress pose two important policy considerations. First, at what level can these problems be attacked? Obviously, some economic maladies are common to large multistate regions. But is there any advantage to a regional organization or program in contrast to direct federal/state or federal/local undertakings? How should federal, state, and local governments share the responsibilities? Does the concentration of needs in the inner city call for a separate urban strategy, bypassing regional or state officials? Finally, can Indian reservations be moved into the economic mainstream or will their federal dependency continue?

A related question concerns the degree to which economic development policy must be multifaceted to accommodate the variety of programs associated with economic growth. To what extent will programs aimed at poor, depressed, rural counties be useful in solving the structural problems of the northeastern states or the growing pains of the West? Over the years policy makers have searched for acceptable criteria to measure need in all situations. Among the most proven indicators of local economic distress are chronic high unemployment, low family incomes, and outmigration. Other well-recognized signs include falling labor-force participation rates, rising dependency ratios, lagging education levels, lack of growth in employment opportunities, low wages, and weakening of local private and government financial bases. Though the symptoms may be the same, the sources of economic depression vary.

Lagging and Growing Counties: 1970

Outmigration and concentration of low income are better indicators of areas with chronic economic problems than an annual unemployment rate. Unemployment may have cyclical and structural roots that may be separated only if the areas are observed over a long period. Migration and income were selected for the purposes of this study to analyze the differences among prosperous and depressed areas.[1]

Federal economic development aid is distributed to units of government, with the county as the basic geographic unit. The 3,141 U.S. counties and their equivalents in 1970 included 448 central city counties or counties that were part of a standard metropolitan statistical area (SMSA) and 2,693 nonmetropolitan counties. To contrast growing and lagging counties in each group, those experiencing net outmigration between 1960 and 1970 were separated from those with positive net migration. To intensify the contrast between lagging and growing areas, nonmetropolitan counties with net outmigration were ranked by their percentage of families with incomes less than $3,000, and those with net migration gains were ranked by their percentage of families with incomes above $10,000. In SMSA counties the income cutoff for those losing population was $4,000. The $3,000 and $4,000 income levels approximate the 1969 poverty lines for farm and nonfarm families of four. The actual thresholds were $3,195 and $3,743, respectively. The U.S. median family income in 1969 was $9,586; therefore, the rich areas are considered to be those with the largest concentrations of families above the median.

The 300 "poorest" lagging non-SMSA counties and the 300 "richest" growing non-SMSA counties—the two extremes—were selected for purposes of contrast. Median family income in the poor group of counties averaged $4,601, compared to $9,174 in the rich ones (Appendix Tables 2A-1 and 2A-2). Similarly, the fifty SMSA counties with negative net migration and the largest proportion of families with incomes under $4,000 were chosen to represent lagging metropolitan areas. SMSA counties gaining population that had the largest proportions of families with incomes of $10,000 or more were identified as growing metropolitan areas. The poor areas averaged a median family income of $7,442; the rich ones $12,692 (Appendix Tables 2A-3 and 2A-4).

Population and Labor Force

Between 1960 and 1970 the population of the United States grew by 13.3 percent. Growth was more rapid in the richer counties, and although some of the counties with negative net migration had population increases as high as 36.6 percent, the mean for the nonmetropolitan areas was −7.8 percent and for metropolitan areas 3.8 percent (Figure 2-1). Moreover, this population loss or slowed growth was occurring among relatively smaller counties. While richer growing nonmetropolitan counties averaged over 50,000 persons, the poorer counties averaged only 14,000. The richest growing metropolitan counties averaged a population of over half a million while the poorest lagging counterparts averaged fewer than 200,000 persons.

The pull to emigrate from lagging areas is sometimes viewed as

28

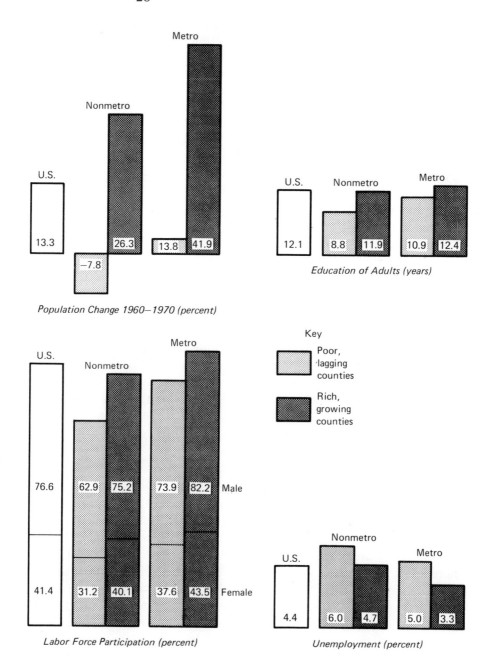

Population Change 1960–1970 (percent)

Education of Adults (years)

Key

Poor, lagging counties

Rich, growing counties

Labor Force Participation (percent)

Unemployment (percent)

Source: U.S. Department of Commerce, Economic Development Administration, *1975 Annual Report* (Washington: Government Printing Office, 1975), in press.

Figure 2-1. Contrasts in Lagging and Growing Areas, 1970.

accelerating the decline by robbing those communities of their more highly skilled segments of the population. Averages for the poor nonmetropolitan counties in the sample appear to bear this out. This suggests that investments in human capital in lagging non-SMSA counties, while crucial for individual welfare, often can have little impact on area growth. Lagging nonmetropolitan counties tend to have greater proportions of elderly and young people among their population than their growing counterparts. Median years of school among those 25 years and over range from just above the U.S. average of 12.1 years to a low of 5.2 in those areas. Lagging metropolitan areas have more elderly among their population than growing ones, but that proportion is somewhat lower than the country as a whole (9.6 percent as opposed to 9.9 percent). Median education levels in the low growth metropolitan counties are below the norm, but tend to be higher than in lagging nonmetropolitan areas.

The most depressed counties are likely to have more than their share of minority groups than the richest growing counties. A fourth of the population in the most depressed nonmetropolitan counties was nonwhite, although the range included many predominantly white counties. The nonmetropolitan sample of the poorest lagging counties includes parts of the Mississippi Delta where outmigration stands at over 30 percent, poverty between 30 and 45 percent, and the nonwhite proportion of population at 60 percent, as well as equally poor and lagging sections of Appalachia, for example, that are almost entirely white.

In both non-SMSA and SMSA growth areas the average nonwhite population was under 5 percent, but the nonmetropolitan areas showed greater variation. The richest metropolitan growth areas all had a nonwhite population of less than 15 percent. These probably represent the expanding suburban rings of the nation's metropolitan areas, largely outside the South, where whites have fled the central cities in large numbers.

The people in growing areas are more likely to be employed than persons in depressed areas. This holds true for males as well as females. Where economic opportunities have declined, labor force participation also drops. Among both males and females, labor force participation in the poor lagging nonmetropolitan counties averages below the national norms. In the richer non-SMSA counties the ranges of participation rates are higher, and the means are closer to the U.S. averages of 41.4 percent for females and 76.6 percent for males. In the urban counties there is a somewhat lesser disparity of labor force participation rates between the rich growing and poor lagging ones. In the lagging SMSA counties, however, labor force participation among men averages only 3.5 percent below the national norm and among women 9 percent below.

A look at the ranges of labor force participation among the four classes of counties suggests that areas of job shortages exist in both metropolitan and nonmetropolitan settings, but that the problem may be more a rural than an urban one. Although these data are based on place of residence rather than workplace, they are likely representative of overall trends since only 17.8 percent of Americans in 1970 worked outside their county of residence. The dispersions in labor force participation in rich growing and poor lagging non-SMSA counties is larger than among their SMSA counterparts. And, in the poorest lagging metropolitan counties, the range in participation is from slightly under the national rate to the average in poor lagging nonmetropolitan areas. The greatest job deficits in metropolitan areas with negative migration are equal to the average situation in the poorest lagging rural counties.

This situation calls for a national policy that recognizes the needs to create jobs both in heavily populated metropolitan areas and less populous nonmetropolitan areas suffering from poverty and outmigration, but not ignoring the fact that job creation is also a problem in some of the richer nonmetropolitan areas. Overall, nonmetropolitan America still trails urbanized areas in growth.

Employment and Unemployment

Manufacturing employment accounts for just over a fourth of U.S. total employment. Although it is usually thought to be an indicator of economic health, the average proportions employed in manufacturing among the four samples of counties differs little, reflecting the wide diversity of productivity and earnings in manufacturing employment. Agricultural employment is a more significant indicator in non-SMSA counties. The poorest lagging nonmetropolitan counties averaged twice the proportion of agricultural employment of the richest growing counties, although the range was large for both groups of counties. As agriculture continues to decline in its share of national employment, the adjustment process will continue to have detrimental effects on some poor nonmetropolitan counties lacking a more diversified economic base.

At the time of the 1970 census, unemployment stood at 4.4 percent, just following a peak in the business cycle. Although there was a great variety of unemployment situations within each sample of counties, on average the lagging areas suffered higher unemployment. It was 6 percent in poor lagging nonmetropolitan areas compared to 4.7 percent in the rich, growing nonmetropolitan counties. The difference in metropolitan areas was slightly greater— 5.0 percent in declining counties and 3.3 percent in those growing.

The wide range of unemployment rates in each instance makes clear that even in good times joblessness is only one measure of economic inadequacy. Unemployment may remain as high as 8 percent in rich and growing metropolitan areas, or even 15 percent in rich and growing nonmetropolitan areas where the adjustment lags behind a rapid growth rate. Low unemployment—down to less than 3 percent in lagging metropolitan areas and less than 1 percent in lagging nonmetropolitan areas may be the result of a long-run adjustment process in which the labor force shrinks as job opportunities are lost. An accurate description of economic need extends beyond a monthly or annual unemployment figure.

The Urban Ghetto

An analysis of lagging metropolitan areas by county masks the more severe problems of ghetto neighborhoods. The 1970 Census Employment Survey of 60 low income areas in 51 cities offers a closer view of inner city poverty pockets (Appendix Table 2A-5). Unemployment and poverty are more severe in these areas, which are more heavily nonwhite than the lagging SMSA counties identified earlier. Labor force participation rates are almost identical, and again are not far below the national average for males. Among women they are actually higher. Moreover, median education levels are high compared with the sample of poor lagging metropolitan counties and stand only slightly below the national norm. Manufacturing employment accounts for slightly over a quarter of the total employment.

Although no measure of net migration is available for these urban neighborhoods, they are likely to represent the most severely depressed subsections of many lagging metropolitan areas. These data tend to support the notion that concentrations of poverty and unemployment in urban areas stem from causes more complex than job shortages. Economic development projects to create jobs may not be as critical a priority in the urban environment as in rural areas. Nonetheless, the need is to lower the barriers to full employment in all areas with wage levels sufficient to raise family incomes above the barest living standard.

The Indian Reservation

Another special case of dire need is the Indian reservation. Although outmigration from the reservations is a continuing process, it is offset by the highest rate of natural increase of any population subgroup in the United States for whom separate data are recorded—3 percent annually. Large families and higher than average death rates skew the age distribution of reservation Indians markedly toward youthful dependents (Appendix Table 2A-6).

Compared to persons in lagging nonmetropolitan areas, reservation Indians were less likely to be in the labor force and far more likely to be unemployed. Median family income in 1969 was $4,088, two-fifths of the white median. The Bureau of Indian Affairs has estimated that for one hundred thirteen reservations surveyed in 1968, almost half of the personal income came directly from the government, either as transfer payments or as wages and salaries for employment in antipoverty, welfare, and other government programs.[2] The potential work force is deficient in education, averaging less than an eighth grade education, and the health of Indians is poor as well. The reservations are located in areas isolated from the economic mainstream. Although the vast tracts of land and their natural resources owned by tribes are the basis of Indian wealth, some have not been fully exploited and most rank low in productivity compared to non-Indian lands. Resource-based activities are compatible with the history and culture of many tribes. Yet, like other rural areas, the percentage of those employed in agriculture has declined sharply during the past decade; in 1970 only one of every ten was employed in agriculture, forestry or fisheries. Despite efforts to encourage private enterprise, government employment has expanded rapidly. In 1970, 46 percent of total employment was in the government sector.[3]

It is not only true that the needs of Indians on reservations are severe, but also that their experience with economic development is severely limited. Fewer than 20 of the over 150 industrial enterprises operating on reservations in 1970 began operations before 1960.[4] Indian planning, managerial, and promotional capabilities are constrained by lack of training and experience as well as cultural values that do not include business development.

Appalachian Economic Distress

During the early 1960s the Appalachian region became synonymous with economic distress, and reacting to a devastating postwar decade of economic decline, a special regional commission was established to focus federal help on its needs. Over two million persons left the area between 1950 and 1960. Employment dropped by 73,000, the number of unemployed rose by 110,000, and others gave up search for employment and dropped out of the work force. Dependence on coal mining and related economic activities had taken its toll on the region both economically and physically. During the 1950s coal production was down by a third and employment in coal fell by two-thirds.[5] As the region is defined today (Map 2-1) three of every ten families lived in poverty in 1960, and almost half of those aged 25 years and over had never gone farther than the eighth grade.

The stereotype of Appalachia as an isolated and backward rural coal mining area is not representative of the region's diversity and the changes that it has undergone over the past decade and a half. Only a quarter of the Appalachian people live in rural counties; half are in metropolitan counties and the rest in other urban counties. Most of the urban and metropolitan areas are in northern and southern Appalachia; Ashland, Kentucky, is the only city with a population in excess of 25,000 in central Appalachia. Metropolitan Appalachia includes several major cities, and on the fringe of the region are other major metropolitan areas, including Atlanta, Cincinnati, Columbus, and Buffalo.

Appalachia experienced a net outmigration of over a million persons between 1960 and 1970, or 6.3 percent of its 1960 population (Appendix Table 2A-7). As was the case in many depressed counties, natural increase more than made up for the loss, and the total population inched up by 2.7 percent during the decade. Metropolitan (SMSA), urban (non-SMSA counties with over 25,000

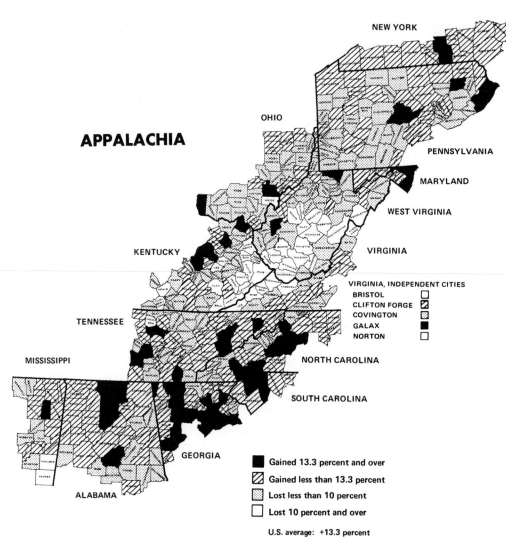

APPALACHIA

VIRGINIA, INDEPENDENT CITIES

BRISTOL	☐
CLIFTON FORGE	▨
COVINGTON	▦
GALAX	■
NORTON	☐

■ Gained 13.3 percent and over

▨ Gained less than 13.3 percent

▦ Lost less than 10 percent

☐ Lost 10 percent and over

U.S. average: +13.3 percent

Source: Map sheet, "Percent Change in Population, by Counties: 1960 to 1970," U.S. Bureau of the Census, 1971.

Map 2-1. Percent Change in Population, by Counties: 1960 to 1970.

inhabitants), and rural Appalachia all had a net outmigration, but the impact was greatest in rural areas and, therefore, in heavily rural Central Appalachia. Throughout Appalachia, rural counties had an outmigration rate of over 11 percent; in central Appalachia it was over 17 percent.

Appalachian poverty in rural and urban areas is within the bounds of the previously defined 300 poor lagging nonmetropolitan counties. However, on average, metropolitan Appalachia has a lower proportion of poverty families than the 50 poor lagging metropolitan areas. As with outmigration, poverty hits rural Appalachia, and therefore central Appalachia, the hardest. Three of every ten central Appalachian families are poor compared with one of every six in the south and one of every ten in the north.

Appalachian poverty is on the decline and at a faster rate than in the nation as a whole. In 1960 the region accounted for a tenth of the nation's population, but 14 percent of its poor, in 1970 one of every eleven Americans lived in Appalachia and an eighth of all the poor. The rate of decrease in the number of poor Appalachian families was highest in urban areas and in the north, although the decline in rural and central Appalachia was substantial as well (Figure 2-2).

Over the decade employment in the region grew slowly at a rate of 11.2 percent, and as a result Appalachia slipped in its share of total employment nationwide from 9 to 8.5 percent. In line with the national trend, agricultural employment was nearly halved. The gains in manufacturing employment occurred in central and southern Appalachia while the north lost ground in manufacturing. Employment in finance, insurance, real estate, and professional services, which occurred throughout the region, were particularly great in the more rapidly growing southern part of Appalachia. Growth in that sector was strong in central Appalachia, but weaker in the northern subregion. These employment trends indicate that northern and southern Appalachia are sharing in the overall trends of their neighboring northeastern and southern U.S. regions. In the former forecasts are that economic growth will be slow; the latter has been building its manufacturing base. Central Appalachia seems to be following the southern U.S. trends but is still held back by its isolation and rural character.

The socioeconomic characteristics of Appalachian people are similar to those in the 300 nonmetropolitan and 50 metropolitan depressed areas. The majority of Appalachian residents, particularly those in rural areas, have not completed high school. Slightly smaller proportions of rural and urban residents are under eighteen and over sixty-five.

But while outmigration and poverty still plague Appalachia, there

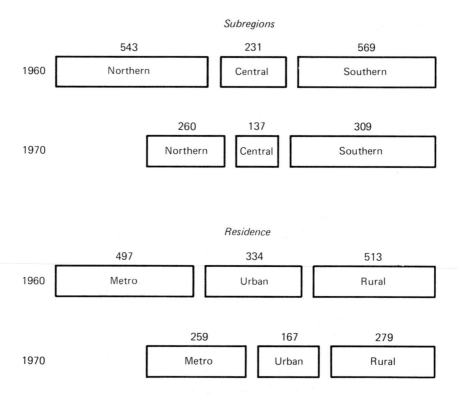

Source: Appalachian Regional Commission, unpublished data.

Figure 2-2. Poor Families in Appalachia, 1960 and 1970 (Thousands).

are some hopeful signs for economic development. Appalachian men outside of the rural areas had higher labor force participation rates than the U.S. average. The unemployment rate in 1970 was below 4.5 percent in metropolitan and urban areas and 5.4 percent in the rural portions of the region. Although during the 1960s Appalachia remained a depressed region, it appears that the massive structural dislocations of the 1950s were being corrected in the 1960s.

Unemployment in metropolitan and urban Appalachian counties appears to have responded to the upturn in the business cycle in 1970, and labor force participation was strong. The impacts of the deeper and more prolonged 1974-1975 recession are not yet fully known. But the recovery in the 1960s notwithstanding, the population remained disproportionately poor (Figure 2-3). One clue might

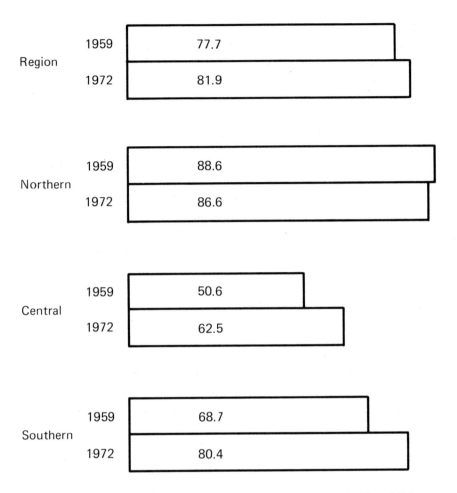

Region
1959 77.7
1972 81.9

Northern
1959 88.6
1972 86.6

Central
1959 50.6
1972 62.5

Southern
1959 68.7
1972 80.4

Source: Jerome Pickard, "Per Capita Income Gap Between Appalachia and U.S. Diminishes," *Appalachia*, June-July, 1975, p. 35.

Figure 2-3. Appalachian Per Capita Income as Percent of U.S., 1959 and 1972.

be found in the apparent underinvestment in education and skill training. Another factor might be the differentially low wage structure of the South. Outmigration and the slow growth of employment may also help to keep incomes low.

Rural Appalachia has these problems compounded. Low labor force participation is likely a result of the failure to retain prime age workers. Unemployment was high despite an upswing in the business cycle. Incomes and educational levels are lower, and poverty is more widespread. In central Appalachia the geographic disadvantages of a rugged terrain and few large population centers continue to militate against new industry.

Local Government Finance

Depressed areas in need of infrastructure to attract industrial development often cannot afford the necessary expenditures. Where physical deterioration lowers property values or keeps them from increasing as rapidly as those in growing areas, property taxes, upon which local governments depend heavily, cannot yield revenues sufficient to support large capital investments. State funds, the other major source of local government revenues generally are tied to specific expenditures: public welfare, education, and highways.

Data compiled by the Appalachian Regional Commission allow a detailed assessment of local government revenues and expenditures in lagging areas.[6] Per capita general revenues available to Appalachian governments averaged just over $210 in 1967, only 71 percent of the national average. They grew less than the national average during the next five years. The locally-raised share of local government general revenues, which was 63 percent nationwide, was only 54 percent in Appalachia.

Federal contributions and local governments follow the Biblical precept that, "For whosoever hath, to him shall be given more in abundance." The federal share of per capita local revenues is the same (4 percent) in all three Appalachian subregions as it is nationwide. Despite federal efforts to help the region, local Appalachian governments receive fewer federal funds per person ($14.32) than the U.S. average ($22.07). In fact the growth of the federal portion of per capita local revenues between 1967 and 1972 was slower in Appalachia than for the country as a whole.

In central Appalachia—the poorest part of the region—local governments have the most difficulty raising money locally—just over $100 per person compared with $169 in southern, and $213 in northern Appalachia, and $318 for the United States. The states appear to bear a greater proportion of the revenue burden in Appalachian counties, and this is especially true in central Appalachia where the state share is 55 percent. This importance of state funds in local government budgets in Appalachia accounts for the fact that Appalachian governments spend slightly larger proportions of their budgets on education, public welfare, and highways than the U.S. average. In general the differences between higher and lower income counties within Appalachia or between central Appalachia and other areas is not reflected in outlays for education because of state aid to public schools.

The Future

The outlook for Appalachia has improved in the early 1970s. Between 1970 and 1973, the population had grown by more than 607,000; this acceleration was marked by a net inmigration of 253,000.[7] Over a third of the returnees were former military personnel and their families. While the impact of reductions in the size of the armed forces is not likely to be repeated, other influences may continue to be important. First, the growth of employment in the southern states and the increased demand for coal to replace foreign energy sources can be expected to attract more persons to Appalachia. The region is experiencing a shortage in coal miners after nearly two decades of surplus. Growing employment is likely the most powerful magnet for inmigration, and the Appalachian highway program hopes to make industrial location more attractive. Second, high unemployment in the urban areas where many migrants of the 1960s settled has historically brought persons home to Appalachia. Also, rising transfer payments, particularly social security and black lung payments, contribute to regional income. Finally, and least certain, is the "back to rural life" movement of young families and retirees.

Appendix 2A:
Economic Indicators in Growing and Lagging Areas

Table 2A-1
Poor, Nonmetropolitan Counties, 1970[a]

Indicators	Mean	High	Low
Change in population, 1960-1970	−7.8%	36.6%	−30.7%
Population, 1970	14,225	80,364	1,340
Labor force participation rate (persons 16 years and over)			
Males	62.9%	80.5%	20.2%
Females	31.2%	48.1%	11.2%
Unemployment rate	6.0%	15.5%	0.3%
Percent of population			
Persons 65 years and over	12.9%	25.5%	4.7%
Persons under 18 years	37.2%	59.5%	24.9%
Persons nonwhite	26.8%	86.5%	0.01%
Median years school (persons 25 years and over)	8.8	12.2	5.2
Percent of families with incomes less than $3,000 (1969)	34.3%	59.9%	0.3%
Median family income (1969)	$4,601	$5,786	$2,407
Percent employed in agriculture (persons 14 years and over)	15,5%	56.9%	0.4%
Percent employed in manufacturing (persons 14 years and over)	21.6%	49.2%	0.0%

[a]300 non-SMSA counties with negative net migration 1960-1970 and largest percentage of families with incomes less than $3,000 in 1969.

Table 2A-2
Rich, Nonmetropolitan Counties, 1970[a]

Indicators	Mean	High	Low
Change in population, 1960-1970	26.3%	234.2%	2.2%
Population, 1970	50,038	583,813	2,365
Labor force participation rate (persons 16 years and over)			
Males	75.2%	90.0%	50.4%
Females	40.1%	60.6%	24.0%
Unemployment rate	4.7%	15.3%	0.9%
Percent of population			
Persons 65 years and over	10.2%	28.6%	2.6%
Persons under 18 years	34.9%	45.7%	22.3%
Persons nonwhite	4.2%	37.4%	0.1%
Median years school (persons 25 years and over)	11.9	14.4	9.1
Percent of families with incomes above $10,000 (1969)	43.8%	72.4%	35.4%
Median family income (1969)	$9,174	$13,433	$7,739
Percent employed in agriculture (persons 14 years and over)	7.8%	45.2%	0.6%
Percent employed in manufacturing (persons 14 years and over)	23.7%	59.2%	0.0%

[a]300 non-SMSA counties with positive net migration 1960-1970 and largest percentage of families with incomes greater than $10,000 in 1969.

Table 2A-3
Poor Metropolitan Counties, 1970[a]

Indicators	Mean	High	Low
Change in population, 1960-1970	3.8%	19.1%	−17.0%
Population, 1970	175,887	1,471,701	12,629
Labor force participation rate (persons 16 years and over)			
Males	73.9%	88.5%	61.1%
Females	37.6%	46.5%	27.2%
Unemployment rate	5.0%	8.0%	2.9%
Percent of population			
Persons 65 years and over	9.6%	17.9%	4.7%
Persons under 18 years	36.0%	44.4%	29.4%
Persons nonwhite	19.1%	47.5%	0.3%
Median years school (persons 25 years and over)	10.9	12.3	7.3
Percent of families with incomes less than $4,000 (1969)	24.5%	42.1%	19.0%
Median family income (1969)	$7,442	$8,622	$4,776
Percent employed in agriculture (14 years and over)	4.8%	20.1%	0.2%
Percent employed in manufacturing (14 years and over)	21.0%	42.9%	5.7%

[a]50 SMSA counties with negative net migration 1960-1970 and largest percentage of families with incomes less than $4,000 in 1969.

Table 2A-4
Rich Metropolitan Counties, 1970[a]

Indicators	Mean	High	Low
Change in population, 1960-1970	41.9%	101.8%	9.8%
Population, 1970	508,952	1,428,080	54,421
Labor force participation rate (persons 16 years and over)			
Males	82.2%	87.6%	71.8%
Females	43.5%	50.3%	36.1%
Unemployment rate	3.3%	8.1%	1.9%
Percent of population			
Persons 65 years and over	7.1%	10.6%	3.1%
Persons under 18 years	36.9%	45.6%	30.1%
Persons nonwhite	4.4%	15.0%	0.3%
Median years school (persons 25 years and over)	12.4	13.0	12.1
Percent of families with incomes above $10,000 (1969)	68.1%	80.0%	61.5%
Median family income (1969)	$12,692	$16,710	$11,596
Percent employed in agriculture (14 years and over)	1.5%	4.9%	0.2%
Percent employed in manufacturing (14 years and over)	27.0%	46.4%	6.7%

[a]50 SMSA counties with positive net migration 1960-1970 and largest percentage of families with incomes greater than $10,000 in 1969.

Table 2A-5
Low Income Urban Areas, 1970[a]

Change in Population, 1960-1970	NA
Total population (thousands)	8,711
Percent of population nonwhite	52.1%
Labor force participation rate (persons 16 years and over)	
Males	73.1%
Females	43.7%
Unemployment rate	9.6%
Percent of families with incomes less than $4,000	27.1%
Median family income	$6,654
Median years school (persons 25 years and over)	12.1
Percent employed in agriculture (persons 16 years and over)[b]	0.0%
Percent employed in manufacturing (Persons 16 years and over)[b]	27.3%

[a]Census Employment Survey's 60 selected areas of 51 cities, totaling 8.7 million persons. The areas selected for the survey were identified first by 1960 Census data and verified by local sources as likely to contain high concentrations of low income persons.

[b]Data available for 16 years and over only.

Source: U.S. Bureau of the Census, Census of Population: 1970, *Employment Profiles of Selected Low Income Areas*, Final Report PHC(3)-1, United States Summary-Urban Areas, January 1972 (Washington: Government Printing Office, 1973), Tables A, C, D, F, I, and 20.

Table 2A-6
Reservation Indians, 1970[a]

Change in population, 1960-1970	NA
Total population (persons 16 years and over)	112,591
Labor force participation rate (persons 16 years and over)	
Males	50.0%
Females	27.2%
Unemployment rate	15.6%
Percent of population	
(persons 65 years and over)	5.5%
(persons under 18 years)	52.4%
Percent of families with incomes less than $3,000	38.5%
Median family income	$4,088
Median years school (persons 25 years and over)	7.6
Percent employed in agriculture (persons 16 years and over)[b]	10.2%
Percent employed in manufacturing (persons 16 years and over)[b]	15.5%

[a]Data for the 110 reservations with largest American Indian populations or approximately one-half the Bureau of Indian Affairs estimate of total reservation population.

[b]Data available for 16 years and over only.

Source: U.S. Bureau of the Census, Census of Population: 1970, *Subject Report: American Indians*, Final Report PC(2)-1F (Washington: Government Printing Office, 1973), Tables 11-14.

Table 2A-7
The Appalachian Region, 1970

Indicators	Region	Metro	Urban	Rural
Change in population, 1960-1970	2.7%	4.4%	4.2%	−1.8%
Labor force participation rate				
Males	79.3	81.8	80.4	73.1
Females	39.7	40.6	41.7	35.7
Unemployment rate	4.5	4.1	4.4	5.4
Percent of population				
Persons 65 years and over	10.5	10.1	10.5	11.1
Persons under 18 years	33.8	33.4	33.3	34.3
Persons nonwhite	NA	NA	NA	NA
Percent of population (persons 25 years and over with less than high school education)	56.2	52.8	54.1	67.0
Percent of families with incomes				
Less than $3,000	14.3	–	–	22.3
Less than $4,000	20.1	16.1	19.5	–
Over $10,000	34.1	40.1	32.6	22.5
Percent employed in agriculture (persons 16 years and over)[a]	3.3	1.7	3.3	7.2
Percent employed in manufacturing (persons 16 years and over)[a]	33.7	32.9	36.3	32.4

[a]Data available for 16 years and over only.
Source: Appalachian Regional Commission, unpublished data.

3 The Chosen Areas

Criteria and Population

The most central issue in economic development assistance is to determine where to concentrate scarce resources. The basic flaw has been the politically expedient course of trying to spread meager loaves among the multitudes. The original measure introduced by Senator Douglas directed aid to industrial labor markets with severe chronic unemployment problems, but rural and smaller urban areas were added to enhance the bill's acceptability. The final criterion, colored by a national unemployment rate that averaged almost 6 percent during the 1958 and 1960 recessions, was a sliding scale based on excess unemployment above the national rate. An area had to average 6 percent unemployment during the preceding year, and either 50 percent above the national average for three of the preceding four years, 75 percent above for two of the last three, or 100 percent one of the last two. The latter measures were based on the notion that persisting high unemployment was a major characteristic of depressed areas. The Area Redevelopment Act administrator was empowered to designate smaller communities on the basis of evidence showing need because of the low income, high unemployment, or outmigration. In addition, Indian reservations qualified for aid. In its first two years ARA designated more than 1,000 counties with about a fifth of the total U.S. population.

Redevelopment Areas

The basic unemployment criteria remained the same when the Area Redevelopment Act was replaced in 1965 by the Public Works and Economic Development Act. Moreover, eligibility was extended on several other bases. An area can qualify as a redevelopment area—eligible to receive assistance under the Act—not only if it meets the unemployment standard, but also if it has a median family income

49

less than half (originally 40 percent) of the national median, if it suffers an unusual and abrupt rise in unemployment expected to reach 50 percent above the national average unless aid is allowed, or if it is an Indian reservation on which the greatest degree of economic distress can be demonstrated. In the unlikely event that no single county qualified, every state could include at least one redevelopment area. Since 1965 special impact areas—communities or neighborhoods with large concentrations of poverty, rural areas with substantial outmigration, or areas with a threatened sudden jump in unemployment to be selected administratively without regard to political boundaries—and areas with a decade-long decline in per capita employment were added to the list.

Once broad eligibility criteria were established, federal administrators were faced with increasingly long lists of the needy. By mid-1975, when unemployment had risen above 8 percent nationwide, 1,794 areas had qualified and, after filing an acceptable economic development plan, 1,590 had been designated for assistance. Half the counties in the United States were eligible to partake in Economic Development Act help. Considering the meager resources Congress made available to the Economic Development Administration, eligibility for assistance did not mean that the agency could deliver help.

Moreover, until 1974 areas with "substantial," i.e., 6 percent, unemployment were eligible for public works grants but not other assistance, even if they failed to meet the "persistence" standards. When the Act was amended in the fall of 1974, Congress broadened the definition of a redevelopment area even further to include all areas with an unemployment rate of 6 percent during the preceding year. The effect was to make those localities previously only able to apply for public works grants eligible for business loans and guarantees. The changes, however, are not backed up with additional funds, potentially spreading thinner the limited resources allocated to aid areas with chronic high job deficits.

Growth Centers

The county-by-county designation of needy areas, while politically convenient, overlooks the fact that these jurisdictions do not necessarily coincide with labor markets or geographic economic entities.

Indeed, many depressed counties are too poor, too small or too isolated to support a growing population and to sustain an economic base. The answer of some regional scientists to these problems is to concentrate assistance at growth centers—places with growth potential where the benefits of increased economic activity can spill over into neighboring depressed areas. Among the advantages of growth centers, it has been argued, are their ability to attract private capital and their larger and more ready labor force. The growth center concept assumes a multiplier effect from investment: wages paid to residents of the center and surrounding area would be recycled in the region's economy, creating more jobs and income. Spurred by these arguments, the drafters of the Appalachian Regional Development Act mandated that investments be concentrated in areas with growth potential. The Public Works and Economic Development Act followed with the establishment of multicounty economic development districts formed around one or more growth centers and at least two redevelopment areas (since modified to one).

Although all counties within the Appalachian boundaries are eligible for commission-supported projects, the law provides that aid must be "concentrated in areas where there is a significant potential for future growth and where the expected return on public dollars invested will be the greatest." The commission accepted the growth area requirement in most cases but made exceptions. Health and education projects can be funded anywhere, with the need to serve the largest number of people more important than location.[1] Access roads to residential, recreation, or education sites, or natural resources projects serving recreation or timber development needs are other examples of exceptions to the growth area orientation.

Since the states are responsible for planning Appalachian investments, they were authorized to designate growth areas. Each state plan differs in its approach to defining growth areas. Most define primary and secondary centers; several use additional categories and delineate the hinterlands to be influenced. The criteria that evolved within the commission were as vague as the legislative mandate for growth areas. The range included areas within the economic sphere of major metropolitan centers both inside and outside Appalachia's boundaries, large Appalachian cities constrained from growth because they lacked land, collections of small towns outside urban areas, areas with dense rural nonfarm populations, and rural areas with unexploited access and resource advantages. The degree to which states were selective in applying these criteria varied.

By January 1976, the Economic Development Administration's planning program included 168 economic development districts encompassing 289 growth centers, 949 redevelopment areas, and 1,310 counties. All but 22 districts received planning assistance from the agency, and 153 were designated for program assistance. To qualify as a development center, the city must be identified in the district's plan, given state approval, and accepted by the agency. By law the lower limit on the size of the centers is 250,000 persons. A much more difficult mandate to interpret is that the centers be linked geographically and economically with the designated needy areas and may, in the words of the law, "reasonably be expected to contribute to the alleviation of distress" in those locations. The established pattern has been that well over half of the growth centers named are not located in redevelopment areas.

Until 1974 only growth centers and designated redevelopment areas were eligible for the Economic Development Act program aid. The 1974 amendments, however, expanded eligibility to cover all areas within the boundaries of economic development districts. The result will be an even further stretching of limited economic development funds since new counties and cities will be added to the list of eligible places if they can show that the project undertaken will help the depressed areas of the district. The provision also adds new incentives to the formation of districts which already include two-thirds of all U.S. counties.

EDA's Target Population

Some 1,300 counties qualified for aid by mid-1973 on the basis of the Economic Development Act's criteria for economic need (Map 3-1). However, another 471 counties that should have been dropped were not because Congress banned dedesignation (Table 3-1). For the purpose of administering the Economic Development Act, Congress has decreed that areas can suffer economic doldrums but not recovery. The Southeast is the major doubtful beneficiary of this policy. The Economic Development Administration's target population of the poor and unemployed living in designated areas is concentrated in the West and Northeast (Table 3-2). Indians on reservations, who represent less than 1 percent of the population of qualified areas, represent one of every seven of the needy in those areas.

Because of the agency's meager resources, it avoided adopting binding criteria for the distribution of its funds. Instead it relied on community and entrepreneurial initiative to apply for aid, and approval was based upon vague standards regarding the quality of proposed projects and their anticipated impact on the target population. The rhetoric of the Economic Development Act also called for scrutinizing the relationship of any proposed project to the overall development plans of the local area. But, as noted, since the overall plans were not necessarily based on any careful study of area needs, the provision to tie specific projects to the area economic plans added to the vagueness of the Economic Development Administration's standards in approving projects.

In fiscal 1975 the agency planned to spend over 40 percent of its public works appropriations and over half of its business development dollars in economic development districts.[2] Urban areas were scheduled to receive less than 30 percent of the funds available under both programs, although in sheer numbers of unemployed their need was greater. Indian reservations and redevelopment areas outside districts were scheduled to receive funds in closer proportion to the numbers of their target population.

The agency has had no firm policy for budget allocations and with relatively little to spend, vast real estate to serve, and a broad mandate, it is not clear that a workable formula for distributing the funds can be designed. By the time any budget is negotiated within the agency, approved by Congress and allocated among the regional offices, the rationale behind a distribution scheme would be barely recognizable. Attempts have been made to spread funds according to total population or target population. Currently, however, the pie is divided by judging the quality of projects and their potential in generating jobs.

The Politics and Economics of Area Designation

From the outset it was clear that the legislative criteria for aid to depressed areas were so broad that funds would have to be spread thinly. The Area Redevelopment Administration recognized more than 1,000 needy counties and obligated a total of $323 million between 1961 and 1965 for distribution among them and their estimated 35 million residents. The Economic Development Administration's cumulative obligations for economic development projects

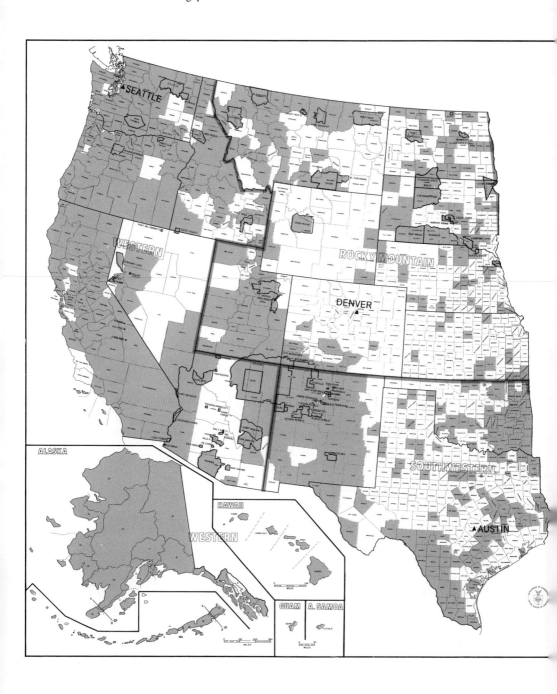

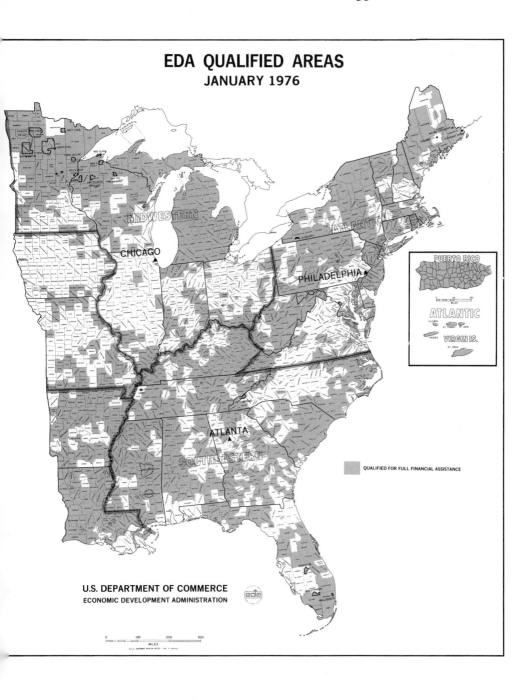

EDA QUALIFIED AREAS
JANUARY 1976

QUALIFIED FOR FULL FINANCIAL ASSISTANCE

U.S. DEPARTMENT OF COMMERCE
ECONOMIC DEVELOPMENT ADMINISTRATION

Table 3-1
Economic Development Act Areas, June 1975

Region	Qualified[a]	Holdover[b]	Designated[c]
Total	1,323	471	1,590
Atlantic	237	21	266
Southeast	192	258	446
Midwest	217	59	209
Southwest	230	75	287
Rocky Mountain	188	51	174
West	259	7	208

[a]Qualified—Areas meeting one of the criteria for EDA assistance.

[b]Holdover—Areas no longer meeting one of the qualification criteria, but still eligible due to congressional ban on dedesignation.

[c]Designated—Areas approved for assistance after filing overall economic development plan.
Source: U.S. Department of Commerce, Economic Development Administration, Office of Planning and Program Support, unpublished data, June 15, 1975.

during its first decade totaled $2.2 billion—almost triple ARA's annual rate. However, the number of qualified areas stood at almost 1,800 with a population of 87 million. As a result, agency officials estimated that only one in five designated areas had received support for a single project each year, which does not ensure that all are served once in five years. Getting subsequent projects becomes easier once local economic development wheels begin to turn.

Under the ever-expanding eligibility criteria, the Economic Development Act has practically ceased to be a program focusing aid on depressed areas. Reliance on the unemployment rate as a measure of economic distress has been widely criticized because of its cyclical nature and because it does not reflect structural problems in local economies. Before the moratorium on dedesignation, about one-third of all areas ever qualified had been terminated, and a fourth had been designated again.[3] In over a third of the cases the labor force was so small that the loss of a few jobs could mean the difference between dedesignation and termination.

Although the elimination of the persistence standards can be attacked on the grounds that too many areas will now qualify as depressed, the formula for persistence may not have been as indicative of economic distress as Congress expected. Because of their structural problems, areas with high unemployment do not

Table 3-2

Distribution of Total and Target Populations in Economic Development Act Areas, 1975

Area or Region	Designated Areas		Qualified Areas	
	Total Population	Target Population	Total Population	Target Population
Total (millions)	71.9	2.7	87.4	3.2
		(percent)		
Type of area	100.0	100.0	100.0	100.0
Districts	22.8	29.2	19.3	25.0
Urban	59.8	40.9	64.1	46.0
Other redevelopment areas	16.8	15.1	16.1	14.3
Indian	0.5	14.7	0.5	14.6
Region	100.0	100.0	100.0	100.0
Atlantic	36.0	23.6	38.5	27.2
Southeast	7.2	12.7	5.9	10.7
Midwest	17.4	13.6	16.4	13.1
Southwest	7.0	11.9	6.7	12.4
Rocky Mountain	4.1	5.4	3.8	5.0
West	28.3	32.8	28.7	31.7

Source: U.S. Department of Commerce, Economic Development Administration, Office of Planning and Program Support, unpublished data, June 15, 1975.

always respond most readily to fluctuations in the national rate. Consequently, one study demonstrated that during the 1960s the number of labor market areas with persistent unemployment was greater in low unemployment years and dipped in times of high national unemployment.[4] Other critics of the unemployment rate as a standard to designate depressed areas point out that high unemployment rates may stem from rapid migration into rich, growing areas as well as from the decline of mature industrial areas, the lack of development in poorer rural areas, or the isolation of the inner city or Indian reservation.

Identifying Growth Centers—The Numbers Game

To identify growth centers accurately is an added problem. Economic Development Act guidelines limited the size of growth centers to areas with a population less than 250,000 people. Spokesmen for larger cities quite naturally objected to the limitation arguing that the larger metropolitan regions are the best bets for continued economic expansion to support inmigration.[5] The agency's own review of the growth centers designated as of 1971 confirmed that a majority had little development potential—in terms of population growth, expanding employment, and a sufficient manufacturing, trade and service employment base.[6]

Conceptual problems aside, the reliability of area unemployment and income data is another concern. In 1971 a General Accounting Office (GAO) report questioned the currency and accuracy of the data used to establish eligibility for economic development assistance and charged that areas of economic distress were not being properly identified.[7] At that time annual average unemployment rates were estimated by state employment services, and data on median income by county were available only from the decennial census.

Following the release of the GAO report the Labor Department shifted responsibility for reviewing the methodology for local unemployment estimation from the Manpower Administration (now the Employment and Training Administration) to the Bureau of Labor Statistics (BLS). Pressures for better estimates mounted during the debate on manpower revenue legislation since it was clear that the formula for the distribution of funds would be based heavily on unemployment. By 1973 BLS began to introduce its improved procedures.[8] The changes included counting the unemployed by residence rather than workplace, allowing for dual jobholding and replacing annual estimates with Current Population Survey data in nineteen states and thirty metropolitan areas. The benefits of better data will accrue to federal agencies interested in economic development, such as EDA and the Appalachian Regional Commission, as well as to the Labor Department for use in distributing funds under the Comprehensive Employment and Training Act. But some states whose unemployment rates were revised downward have attacked the new system and have taken their case to the courts. Future improvements may be forthcoming as work at BLS continues, including perhaps an expanded Current Population Survey sample for more extensive coverage and greater accuracy.

Although the Office of Business Economics (now the Bureau of Economic Analysis) at the Department of Commerce began to develop total and per capita personal income and earnings data for local areas in 1967, the GAO study considered these data unreliable for small regions. Census data, collected from families, include only cash income whereas the personal income data are compiled from business and government records plus estimates of imputed income. The GAO reported in 1971 that census officials believed the personal income series could be improved to yield yearly estimates. However, at present the Economic Development Administration is still reluctant to adopt data that lack the confidence of the Congress and the public.

The need for accurate local labor force and income data has been recognized, but was of little operational significance to the Economic Development Administration as long as Congress consistently followed a policy of expanding eligibility. Congress may evidence greater interest to ensure reliability of the data if, as under the Comprehensive Employment and Training Act, and the Housing and Community Act, the distribution of funds is made to depend on these data.

The place-of-residence concept is designed to identify the target population by political jurisdiction while the place-of-work concept focuses on the area's ability to create jobs. The differences could be significant on a county-by-county basis, but if measured on a labor market basis, the two concepts should give equal weight as to need. For the purpose of defining need by single counties, the former definition could be judged more desirable on the grounds that it measures the economic health of the area, and the Economic Development Act's aid is location-oriented. From the vantage point of creating multicounty economic development districts, however, the new definition is better since it attempts to locate the people in need and does not confine aid to the geographic jurisdiction where they live, but allows projects in growth centers.

Designation Dilemmas

The problems of economically depressed areas are far more varied and complex than high unemployment and low median family income. Low rates of labor force participation, low levels of educational attainment and concentrations of minorities, for example, suggest that job creation alone will not solve the problems of declining areas. The challenge is to create jobs paying decent wages, but this requires skill training, effective enforcement of antidiscrimination, and special efforts to make the areas attractive for new economic activity.

Depressed areas range from small isolated rural communities to sections of large metropolitan areas. Most of the Economic Development Act target population resides in urban areas, although the number of depressed nonmetropolitan counties far outweighs the metropolitan ones. If the goal were to serve as many people as possible, concentrating aid in urban areas would be most efficient. However, needs may be most severe in small, isolated rural areas and particularly on Indian reservations. A policy to limit help to the most depressed areas would serve the people stranded in those regions first.

Whatever the policy, limited economic development funds can be spread only so thin before choices must be made among lagging areas. The current criteria for designation, then, appear far too loose as standards for assistance, but Congress has chosen to qualify even more areas and has proscribed striking any from the list. Any alternative criteria for designation necessarily would be arbitrary, and dependence on the unemployment rate is dictated by technical considerations. Nevertheless, consideration should be given to tightening the legislative definition of a depressed area or at least to promote actively projects in the most depressed areas.

Economic need can be measured on many levels. While attacking problems on a labor market basis is perhaps most logical from an economic point of view, the constraints of political boundaries make it difficult to implement. To the extent that the formation of economic development districts involves combining areas with economic ties, districts are preferred to a county-by-county approach. Within the districts, however, aid must be directed at the needy, and the selection of growth centers must be more than an excuse to locate projects outside redevelopment areas. If the benefits of growth center projects are not reaching the target population, consideration should be given to restricting aid to designated redevelopment areas.

The role for regional economic development organizations is less clear. Even economic dislocations shared regionwide must be attacked locally. The benefits of cooperation among governors, and between the state houses and local city and county development organizations must be weighed; but given the variety of local needs within a multistate region, regional decision-making must not become so generalized as to become insensitive to local needs.

4 Economic Development Organizations: Links in the Federal Chain

Planning Requirements and Practices

Perhaps the least controversial provision of the Area Redevelopment Act of 1961 was the requirement that a community seeking eligibility for funds had to prepare an overall economic development program, which was subject to both state and agency approval. The naive hope was that the preparation of the plans would generate economic expansion and that each subsequent request for Area Redevelopment Act funds would be consistent with this plan. Despite the failure of most plans to fulfill the ideal of "blueprints for progress" during the relatively brief history of the Area Redevelopment Act, planning requirements were retained and, in fact, broadened in the Public Works and Economic Development Act and the Appalachian Regional Development Act of 1965.

Although the Area Redevelopment Act pioneered in the establishment of community planning organizations under a federally-funded program, the concept of economic development planning was not new to many depressed areas. A survey prepared by the Committee for Economic Development prior to the passage of the Act identified 14,000 local development groups.[1] While many were paper organizations, over 4,500 were publicly financed, mostly planning and zoning boards, and others received private support, largely from local chambers of commerce and related organizations. Industrial promotion was the most common activity of these groups; research and comprehensive economic development planning were rare.

It was not surprising, therefore, that Area Redevelopment Act committees had little trouble finding local organizations to prepare overall economic development programs (OEDP), although the documents normally lacked quality and depth. Area Redevelopment Administration policy makers chose not to let inadequate plans impede financial assistance, and the OEDPs were modified and progress reports submitted in response to agency critiques. In some cases the agency applied technical assistance funds to help communi-

61

ties prepare their OEDPs. The development and review of 1,000 OEDPs could not receive priority in an agency severely short on funds and personnel, and OEDP planning in many cases failed to advance beyond the prerequisite-for-funding stage.

Economic Development Act Planning

The Economic Development Act retained the requirement that OEDPs be prepared and accepted before final designation for aid. The agency makes planning grants to support the writing of plans and the administration and operation of local development organizations. Most of the planning aid has been allocated to localities participating in economic development districts where individual county planning has become subsumed under district OEDPs. The Economic Development Administration is scheduled to fund 144 districts during fiscal 1977 at a cost of $6.3 million.[2] In contrast, only eight redevelopment areas outside district boundaries were scheduled to receive agency assistance to support the activities of local economic developers. It believes there are economies of scale in funding districts and hopes to include less populous redevelopment areas in new districts as funds become available. In addition, the agency allocated $3.7 million for administrative support to seventy-two of one hundred fifty designated Indian reservations and Alaskan native villages.

The Economic Development Administration's emphasis on district planning grew out of disappointment with the Area Redevelopment Administration's county-by-county approach to planning and funding projects. Preceding the Economic Development Act, the Appalachian Regional Commission was authorized to support the formation of multicounty local development districts. The Economic Development Act districts were to be directly related to the goal of identifying growth centers and linking their planning with that of redevelopment areas. The President's Appalachian Regional Commission outlined other justifications for the multicounty approach, including the advantages of pooling ideas and resources as well as the need for local representation in determining how federal dollars would be used locally.

Both pieces of legislation intended that these substate districts be created with the approval of the governor and that they be nonprofit organizations broadly representative of the interests of elected officials and the public. Parallel guidelines for funding development district staff also were established· either agency could contribute 75 percent of a district's administrative budget; the rest was to be raised locally. That the district programs of the two agencies overlapped in Appalachia was recognized at the outset, and as the formation of districts in Appalachia proceeded, a single organization served the purposes of both agencies. Most districts are organized as public bodies although five nonprofit private bodies are included in the sixty-nine districts. Enabling legislation or an executive order from the state capital is necessary in order to establish a statewide system of districts.

Funds to operate districts are provided by all three levels of government. A survey of economic development districts showed that they received $71 million in 1975, mostly from federal agencies, but the Economic Development Administration's contribution was less than 10 percent of the total and the Appalachian Regional Commission's about 6 percent (Table 4-1). Local contributions accounted for over 15 percent and state for over 5 percent of the total. The sixty-nine local development districts in Appalachia received their $29 million from different sources than the economic development districts. The commission provided about 15 percent of

Table 4-1
Sources of Administrative Funding for Economic and Local Development Districts, 1975
(In millions)

Source	EDA	ARC
Total	$71.2	$29.1
Federal	56.3	25.7
EDA	(6.7)	N.A.
ARC	(3.6)	(4.3)
Other	(45.9)	(21.4)
State	3.9	2.0
Local	11.0	1.4

Note: Some EDA economic development districts are also ARC local development districts. The data are based on two surveys: one by the Office of Development Organizations, Economic Development Administration, U.S. Department of Commerce, and the other by the Office of Program Support and State and LDD Coordination, Appalachian Regional Commission.

the funds, states 7 percent, and local jurisdictions about 5 percent. But there, too, other federal funds gave the major support to the districts.

The Departments of Health, Education, and Welfare, Labor, Housing and Urban Development, and Justice topped the list of other federal contributors. In the economic development districts, almost $10 million HEW dollars supported program grants for the aging and practically all of the Justice Department's $5 million were expended for Law Enforcement Assistance Administration projects. The Labor Department contribution includes a single $6 million project in its $14 million of aid.

HUD's comprehensive (so-called 701) planning grants accounted for $7.2 million in 130 districts. These grants, like the basic Economic Development Administration and Appalachian Regional Commission resources available for administering the districts, help pay for the staff and preparation of plans or project applications. The 701 program, begun in 1954, became part of the 1974 Housing and Community Development Act, under which block grants for water, sewer, public facilities, and other community development efforts are made to local jurisdictions. For districts to meet the HUD requirements for planning funds, two-thirds of the board members must be local elected officials and the organization cannot incorporate. These restrictions do not impede district activities to a great extent, but like Economic Development Administration and Appalachian Regional Commission standards, influenced the composition of these substate planning bodies.

The state and local contributions to the districts are an indication of the potential viability of these bodies. The state contribution is appropriated by the legislature from general funds either the same amount per district or on a formula basis. Local shares are collections from participating governments on a per capita basis. In Appalachia they vary from two to twenty-five cents per person; the Economic Development Administration estimates twenty-five cents per person is the district norm. The local share in some districts is partly in-kind as well. At the present rate nonfederal support of a district averages less than $100,000 annually. Although state support has been growing, most districts are not likely to survive without continued federal aid unless they receive even more vigorous state support in the future.

Alternatively, the viability of the districts may be judged by their success in obtaining a variety of funding sources and not serving just one federal master. Two of every three economic development districts in 1971 had more than one source of federal funds outside the Economic Development Administration; by 1975 that proportion had risen to over 90 percent.[3] The average economic development district has about seven outside grants from five agencies and an annual budget close to $500,000. Appalachia's local development districts have similar budgets and a variety of funding sources as a result, no doubt, of the Appalachian Regional Commission format of supplementing the funding of existing federal programs.

Although the geographic boundaries of the Economic Development Administration's economic development districts and Appalachia's local development districts may coincide, the agencies differ in their view of the districts' role in the federal/state/local partnership. The Appalachian Regional Commission was established at the urging of those who believed a multistate partnership with the federal government could best revitalize the region. Although districts and localities would be eligible to receive commission funds, the philosophy was that the states were in the best position to identify needs and to set priorities.

In contrast, the Economic Development Administration's grant and loan procedures followed more closely the federal/local route, by-passing the states, which was common to many Great Society programs. Like the Appalachian districts, the economic development districts had to be formed under enabling legislation or under an executive order from the state capital. Nonetheless, the Economic Development Administration did not originally foster state planning and cooperation with the districts. Until 1974 federal funds for economic development planning at the state level came either from Appalachia or from one of the other Title V regional commissions. The 1974 Economic Development Act amendments included a new provision for economic development grants to states (as well as districts, redevelopment areas, counties and cities) that cooperate with districts and localities in economic planning. The grants are intended to encourage states and substate districts to work together and are a supplement to the grants for administering districts provided annually by the Economic Development Administration.

District Planning

The Appalachian and Economic Development Administration approaches to district planning differ largely because of the contrasting views of the district's role. Each of the Economic Development Administration's economic development districts, as well as redevelopment areas outside districts, must file an acceptable overall economic development program (OEDP)—a document describing the district's economic development plans. The content is expected to include economic self-analysis, agreed-upon goals, suggested actions, and a description of the community organization. The results normally are long on socioeconomic data, frequently of doubtful relevance, and short on the development of a strategy to implement the goals. In many cases, the goals are "wish-lists" or backlogs of projects that community leaders have kicked around for years. These documents are not applications for funding and do not commit resources; they only establish eligibility for Economic Development Act funds. Therefore, they are often prepared by the staff, consultants or local college professors without significant contributions by the community board membership.

Appalachian local development districts, on the other hand, initiate sets of project proposals that are sent to the state for inclusion in the state plan and project package submitted to the commission. The commission encourages the type of research needed for an OEDP, but does not require the submission of a formal document. In fact, since most local development districts serve as economic development districts, such a requirement would be superfluous.

The relationship between state plans prepared in Appalachia and local district plans has depended largely on the method of organization chosen by the governors. A 1971 review of state planning activities found that local development districts contributed in only a few cases to state plans.[4] As governors have become involved in strengthening state government, however, departments for state planning, budgeting or coordinating federal programs have become more popular. The payoff for both Appalachian and other economic development districts is better coordination and a more unified voice in Washington.

Local Involvement

In both Appalachian and economic development districts, the quality of planning is not as significant a measure of success as the involvement of local elected officials and citizens in the programs. Elected officials usually form a majority on development district boards of directors, and the private sector representation normally is recruited from the ranks of businessmen, bankers, labor groups, and civic leaders. Most, then, are representatives of the local establishment. The Economic Development Administration requires minority representation on the boards and staffs proportional to the population, and a 1972 survey showed that 10 percent of board members nationwide were minority group representatives. Minority membership on the boards may have some influence on the direction of local activities, but not be as significant a determinant of the degree to which minorities will benefit from economic development projects. The type of projects available and the degree to which positive action is taken to ensure that minorities are hired are more important in determining employment of minorities.

Early evaluations of the economic development districts (and other areas receiving Economic Development Act funds) concluded that vigorous leadership, usually due to a strong executive director, characterized the most effective districts.[5] The lack of grassroots support did not trouble the evaluators as long as local businessmen, civic leaders, and government officials lent their support. A similar pattern of local involvement characterized the early years of local development districts.[6] By 1975 an Economic Development Administration official warned that one-man dominance of the board of directors can cause a district to turn sour. For that reason, the use of committees and as much community exposure as possible is encouraged.

Practicing the art of federal grantsmanship is the first and, in many cases, the main function of the districts. Few actually become involved in program operation. The districts that function best, according to both Economic Development Administration and Appalachian officials, are selective in the grants they seek or attempt to find money to match their planned priorities. Without denigrating this statesmanlike approach, one Appalachian Regional Commission staffer suggested that the districts that are deemed to be the most successful attract the largest number of federal grants. Broadening their services to the participating communities is another measure of district achievement. The staffs of some districts have become floating management consultants able to provide technical assistance on nonproject problems.

Looking Ahead

Economic development districts and local development districts serve several purposes. First, both the Economic Development Act and the Appalachian Regional Development Act promoted the formation of districts to stimulate local involvement in programs to be supported largely with federal funds. The Economic Development Administration put more emphasis on planning at the outset and stressed the need for local boards to study their area's development problems in order to foster local participation. The Appalachian Regional Commission concentrated less on formal plans and more on specific project proposals. Both, however, looked ahead to a time when district organizations would play a more significant role in local affairs and would coordinate under their umbrellas a variety of federal efforts. As the districts have already collected a number of federal grants under their purview, they may realize these anticipations.

Another potential source of influence for the districts is the review process known by its bureaucratic designation as A-95. Initiated in 1969 by the Bureau of the Budget, the predecessor to the Office of Management and Budget (OMB), under the 1968 Intergovernmental Cooperation Act, the procedure requires federal agencies to notify and invite comments from state-designated clearinghouses before undertaking a project in the jurisdiction. The review boards can be state agencies, councils of governments or regional planning bodies. Nearly 100 federal programs require an A-95 signoff. Where local officials have given development district boards this power, the districts have the advantage of advance knowledge about prospective efforts related to their own activities. As of early 1975, about six of ten districts held such review authority and could therefore prepare to consider the new projects in planning their operations.

Are these district organizations viable? The answer depends largely on whether state and local funds would be forthcoming to replace federal support. Such funding would likely be available most readily to districts that have established an ability to serve state and local government purposes as well as the federal government. Planning has gained considerable respectability in public administration, but whether economic district planning organizations would survive without active federal help is debatable. Between 1952 and 1972 the number of special substate districts in the United States responsible for planning a wide range of federal and state programs almost doubled, to 23,866.[7] The problem may turn out to be not the lack of support for economic development districts, but one of coordinating these special purpose agencies that have received growing federal, state, and local encouragement.

Regional Commissions

Counties and contiguous multicounty areas are not necessarily self-sufficient economic entities. To satisfy members of Congress from other regions who lent their support to the Appalachian program, the 1965 Public Works and Economic Development Act provided for the establishment of regional development commissions. Five were designated in 1966—Ozarks, New England, Upper Great Lakes, Four Corners, and Coastal Plains—and two were added in 1972—Old West and Pacific Northwest. The commissions comprise all or part of 31 states (Map 4-1).

No new program funds were earmarked for the so-called Title V commissions, and the Bureau of the Budget (now Office of Management and Budget) envisioned them as planning groups to function like the President's Appalachian Regional Commission, the study group preceding the establishment of the Appalachian Regional Commission.[8] Therefore, during their first two years of existence, the Secretary of Commerce was authorized only to supply them with technical assistance and administrative funds. The commissions anticipated more than promises and proposed program funding, but each year's requests have shrunk significantly on their way from the commission to the Department of Commerce to the Office of Management and Budget to the congressional appropriations committees. In 1967 Congress authorized the commissions to provide supplemental grants for other federal projects and in 1969 demonstration grants, but between 1967 and 1975, the commissions were able to obligate only about $260 million for their activities.

Regional Need

The argument for multistate regional commissions is that regionwide economic problems can best be attacked through the cooperation of

70

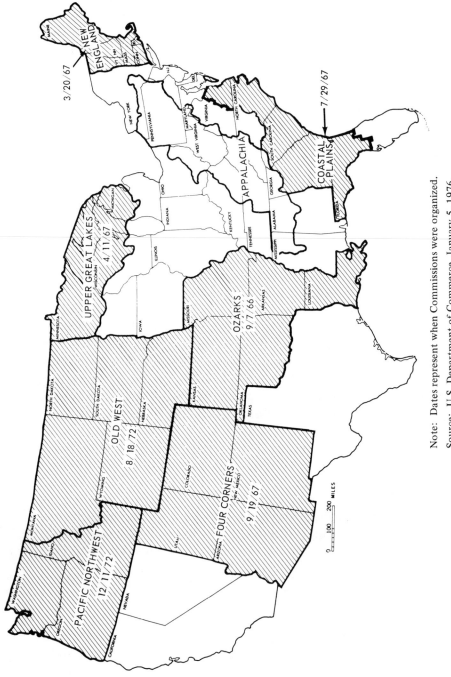

Note: Dates represent when Commissions were organized.

Source: U.S. Department of Commerce, January 5, 1976.

Map 4-1. Economic Development Regions.

federal and state governments with the federal government supplying the funds. The ground rules for drawing regional boundaries called for the areas to be related by geography, history, and economic conditions. Moreover, they had to lag behind national economic development standards measured by unemployment levels, family income, living standards, outmigration, low growth rates, decline of a dominant industry, and adversely changing technology or loss of national defense facilities.

Each region can cite regionwide problems. In New England they are largely due to shifts in plant location and changing composition of national demand for manufactured goods. Along the Coastal Plains regional problems stem from a history of a scattered rural population previously dependent on agriculture and recently able to attract only low wage industry. The Ozarks is an underdeveloped area with relatively unproductive agriculture, an unskilled labor force, outmigration of its youth, and shortages of capital. The fringes of the Upper Great Lakes, once dependent on agriculture, forestry and fishing, have seen their paper mills move south and west and agriculture decline leaving behind an older, scattered, and isolated labor force. Lack of linkages with markets outside the region also plague the Four Corners area of the Southwest. Adapting to the decline of agriculture has been a problem for the upper Missouri River states of the Old West Region. Finally, the Pacific Northwest faces the problems of rapid population expansion, but lower income and higher than national unemployment as well as a desire to control the environmental quality impede economic development.

The commissions were conceived as a means of identifying region-wide problems, and their proposals for action were to alleviate those needs. However, most commission funds are spent on projects with a limited impact area. The New England Regional Commission plan, in fact, presses the belief that regional problems stem from imbalances in subareas of the region that have different economic needs.[9]

Commission Activities

The activities of the commissions are constrained not only by a shortage of funds, but also by the enabling legislation. Their supplemental grants may be spent only on federal programs for the acquisition of land, or construction and equipment, or facilities. The regional commissions are designed, then, to concentrate on helping localities within the region attract grants for highways, airports, vocational schools, industrial sites, water and sewer lines, or other public facilities. Few such programs—with the possible major exception of transportation—have a regional impact. Technical assistance funds account for a smaller portion of each commission's expenditures, but can be used to serve the goal of developing cooperative regional outlooks. Several cite regionwide studies—for example, the Coastal Plains' deepwater terminal study or the Four Corners projects on air service in the region—but most technical assistance funds support more localized studies. Other funds are allocated for regional economic analysis, state planning, and to provide services to state governments.

Viability of the Regional Approach

The Title V regional commissions have had a difficult time winning recognition or achieving visibility. The programs to which the commissions lend support normally are initiated by states or localities. Officials at these levels do not usually seek commission advice, just supplemental funds. And, since the federal grants remain subject to the criteria set by the agency providing the basic funds, preference in meeting commission goals is likely coincidental.

If the commissions can have only a limited impact on the location of projects through supplemental grants, does the federal/state partnership have other meaningful influences on ameliorating regional problems? Proponents believe there are economies of scale in supporting a staff for planning and information on a regional level and that national problems can be investigated through the federal/ commission/state system.[10] The retarded growth of existing commissions have caused them to be ignored or not taken seriously by governors and federal agencies in the past. Their activities are not likely to lend much guidance to future economic development policy, although the potentials of improved interstate and intergovernmental cooperation remain. Nevertheless, the Title V commissions are struggling to develop political clout and have secured an endorsement from the National Governors' Conference, which has proposed a nationwide network of multistate regions and substate districts as a means of improving federal economic development programs. A bill to put the Title V commissions on equal footing with the Appalachian Regional Commission and to give them more money was introduced in the Senate during the summer of 1975. Under this proposal, the commissions would be allocated approximately $250 million annually to support demonstration projects devoted to energy, health, and vocational education.

Technical Assistance

Technical assistance is closely related to the planning activities to stimulate lagging areas. At the time the Area Redevelopment Act was drafted, technical assistance funds were thought to be crucial to developing the potential resources of depressed areas and studying ways to eliminate bottlenecks in area economic expansion. Although these goals had a long-run planning flavor, the technical assistance program that evolved supported undertakings with a more short run impact: potential studies of feasibility, marketing and tourism, for example. The basic thrust of the Economic Development Act's technical assistance is much the same. Funds are available to a wide range of public and private development organizations, universities, and national associations to study, plan, and manage economic development. Technical assistance dollars also have been used for demonstration projects, as operating funds for vocational schools and, more recently, for firms hurt by competition from foreign trade. Technical assistance is not limited to designated areas, but can be given to any area that the agency determines has substantial need.

Technical assistance funds may cover the total cost of services and up to 75 percent of the administrative costs of projects. Although some studies undertaken each year may cost less than $10,000, the average cost of the projects funded between fiscal 1966 and 1974 is over $40,000 (Table 4-2). Among the more costly projects (those over $100,000) are operating funds for several training facilities and planning grants in areas threatened by defense closings. The types of projects that can qualify for technical assistance vary widely, and over the years needs and priorities have changed. Lately, helping local economies adjust to trade and defense closings has become an important consideration. This activity, for example, accounted in fiscal 1974 for seventy-nine projects at a cost of $7.6 million. An illustration is the study prepared on the reuse of a closed Air Force

Table 4-2
Technical Assistance Projects and Outlays, Fiscal 1966 to 1975

Classification	Number	Costs (millions)
Total	2,903	$119.9
Economic data and studies	766	30.1
Management assistance	446	12.8
Site industrial feasibility	300	21.3
Tourism and recreation	163	3.2
Area industrial feasibility	126	3.8
Education	154	10.3
Human resources	114	8.9
Other	774	29.4

Note: Details may not add to totals due to rounding.
Source: U.S. Department of Commerce, *1975 Annual Report Economic Development Administration* (Washington: Government Printing Office, 1976), in press.

base in Laredo, Texas. It offered several innovative suggestions: conversion of flight facilities to a municipal airport, of the hospital to a mental retardation center, and of the dental clinic to a training facility for the local junior college, as well as development of an industrial park and commercial complex. Technical assistance grants can make planning easier, but it is clear that Laredo has a long way to go in restoring the estimated 2,200 jobs lost when the base closed.

The Economic Development Administration funded a feasibility study on the use of solar energy for air conditioning Puerto Rican factories. Memphis State University received help in administering a training program for nuclear power plant technicians, and Colorado State offered a seminar to acquaint architects and engineers with solar energy projects. Productivity and the quality of life are "in" as well. In addition to several grants to academia to study these problems, the agency has funded one by Work in America, a nonprofit organization of labor and management.

Rail abandonment is another economic change that has brought requests for technical assistance funds. In such instances the Economic Development Administration has been criticized as being unable to act in anticipation of adverse economic changes, and the best help the technical assistance program could provide was to study means to reverse down trends. In 1974 Title IX was added to the law to earmark funds for grants as well as technical assistance in hopes of expanding and improving economic adjustment efforts.

Technical assistance has been used to help Indians. The American Indian Management Institute and the American Indian Travel Commission are EDA-funded, and under the new emphasis on promoting tribal planning and managerial skills, technical assistance funds may help in building the development potential on reservations.

Feasibility Studies

The funding of studies to determine the potentials of industrial development and tourism or recreation projects has been a well-established function of the technical assistance program since Area Redevelopment Administration days. Too frequently there is no follow up to recommendations that flow from the feasibility studies. Of 101 feasibility studies with positive recommendations completed during 1966 and 1967, 40 were followed by promotional activities and 24 got as far as financial investments; for 17 no money could be found.[11] Industrial projects had better follow-up records than tourism, public facilities, and natural resources. A more recent survey of forty-six tourism and recreation studies was discouraging.[12] It found many of the studies lacking in a full-fledged consideration of the project from selection of the project from among alternatives, through demand and cost analysis, to plans for implementation. In only eighteen of forty-two cases where implementation was recommended had it begun or is planned in the near future.

Institution Building

Throughout the history of technical assistance program the support of institutions involved a wide range of economic development activities has been a major component of the program. Before the creation of the Office of Minority Business Enterprise in 1969, Economic Development Administration technical assistance made a significant contribution to the support of national minority business development organizations. These national organizations and their local chapters help minority businessmen to negotiate loans and advise them on advertising, marketing, accounting, and other aspects of establishing and operating their enterprises. A 1971 study of several of these projects reported that not only did the need continue for the Economic Development Administration to support such organizations since most appeared unable to gain financial independence, but in most cases where the directors provided vigorous leadership and sufficient funds were available to allow them to offer quality staff assistance, the organizations were providing necessary and visible services.[13]

National organizations like the National Center for Urban Ethnic Affairs and local chapters of groups like the Black Economic Union continue to receive support from the Economic Development Administration. Local nonprofit organizations also are funded, including the Economic Resources Corporation, which is promoting an industrial park for minority businesses in Watts, or New Extentions for Utilizing Scientists, whose aim is to have former defense and space science technicians use their technical expertise in advising small businesses on modern technological applications.

The technical assistance program also has promoted economic development centers associated with colleges and universities. Centers hold seminars, make surveys, conduct feasibility studies, and provide managerial counseling. Some work directly with economic development districts and Indian tribes. Reports from several centers on their 1974 activities assert that the free helping hand is well utilized. The University of Utah, for example, claimed to be involved in the creation of over 1,500 jobs and the saving of 300 more in rural sections of the state over a two and one-half year period. The University of Tennessee center reached out to over ninety firms in which almost 1,200 new jobs were added and 400 saved. Whether the Economic Development Administration can take full credit for these jobs is, of course, subject to debate as other factors and funds were no doubt important. But since the lack of managerial and technical skills is a barrier to many business ventures and since the costs of marketing and feasibility studies are likely to be prohibitive for businessmen in needy areas, these projects, which cost less than $100,000 annually, are probably a worthwhile investment.

Education and Manpower Training

As mentioned earlier, the Economic Development Administration's technical assistance program has provided operating funds for several training institutions built with the agency's public works support. In 1974 almost $2.1 million was spent on nineteen education projects. The larger grants support Opportunities Industrialization Centers—in Alabama, San Jose, and Seattle, for example—but smaller projects like a $65,000 grant to the Immigrants Development Center of San Francisco to train new Chinese immigrants as chefs, or a $45,000 grant to Oakland's Project Upgrade to train minority construction workers were included among the training projects.

Today's employment and job training programs for the unemployed, underemployed, and poor have their roots in the first economic development bill. Although federal aid for vocational training dates back to 1917, architects of the Area Redevelopment Act felt it was imperative to provide funds to upgrade the skills of the jobless and to retrain workers whose skills have become obsolescent and who live in depressed areas in order to attract new businesses. Since then, manpower programs have shifted their focus from overcoming changes in skills accompanying technological advance to the needs of the poor, deficiently educated, and unskilled, largely independent of economic development efforts.

With the enactment of the Manpower Development and Training (MDTA) of 1962, skill training similar to that of the Area Redevelopment Act programs was made available nationwide. The Area Redevelopment Administration continued to operate its programs separately until 1965 when it was replaced by the Economic Development Administration. At that time, the MDTA was amended, and the job training program for depressed areas became Section 241 of the manpower law.

Over the next eight years there was little difference in the quality or content of regular MDTA institutional and on-the-job training programs and those aimed at depressed areas.[14] While the Departments of Labor and Health, Education and Welfare argued for more flexible use of the funds, the Economic Development Administration pressed for guaranteed access to Section 241 monies. The agency complained to Congress during the course of the congressional review of the agency that the Department of Labor used 241 funds for non-Economic Development Act projects and that unavailability of funds hindered Economic Development Administration operations.[15] However, Congress would not agree to a separate Economic Development Administration manpower budget, insisting that the two federal agencies should be able to cooperate. The interagency problems marred the program until it ended.

The case for training funds as magnets for prospective businesses was weak with the exception of some on-the-job training projects. Nevertheless, the largely rural redevelopment areas benefited from the more flexible eligibility and allowance created under Section 241. More important, however, as the Labor Department shifted its attention to urban problems, the Section 241 program was the primary source of training funds for some smaller areas.

With the passage of the 1973 Comprehensive Employment and Training Act (CETA), the separate program for redevelopment areas ended. Since CETA funds are to be distributed on the basis of a formula to all cities and counties with over 100,000 population to be used for local priorities, the allocation of manpower funds for economic development projects depends on local planning. Proponents of a separate manpower fund for economic development purposes argue that planning is a major barrier since priorities must be budgeted almost two years ahead. Thus, it is unlikely that funds will be available or that projects could be synchronized with, for example, the completion of an industrial park. Moreover, many redevelopment areas are too small to have their own planning councils and now are dependent on the state for manpower services.

5

The Appalachian Program

The Appalachian Regional Commission is the only regional economic development planning institution given both form and substance. Unlike its Economic Development Act counterparts that remain largely paper organizations, the Appalachian Regional Commission has had at its disposal between 1966 and 1975 a staff of 110 persons in Washington, which has gained its independence from federal executive direction, control over a $1,504 million highway program, and another $1,043 million to allocate to the thirteen states for various government programs. Along with its control over federal funds, the commission has garnered political clout and unwaivering support in Congress, which combine to make it an active and influential regional agency (Map 5-1).

Appalachian policies and actions are decided by a commission composed of a federal cochairman named by the President and the thirteen Appalachian governors or their alternates named from cabinets or personal staffs. Decisions require the approval of the federal cochairman and a majority of the states. This commission meets quarterly. Day-to-day operations are the responsibility of the executive director who heads the staff, the federal cochairman, and states regional representative. This latter position is unique to the Appalachian Regional Commission because the states decided to hire a full-time watchdog to ensure that the commission did not drift into becoming another federalized Washington bureaucracy. Until 1976 the approval of state plans and projects as well as many financial and administrative responsibilities not delegated to the executive director could be decided by the agreement of the federal cochairman and state regional representative (the executive director has no vote) between commission meetings. The amendment approved by President Ford on December 31, 1975 required a quorum of state members to approve Appalachian Regional Commission policy decisions and projects.

Project recommendations prepared by the commission staff are circulated to the state's regional representative and the federal

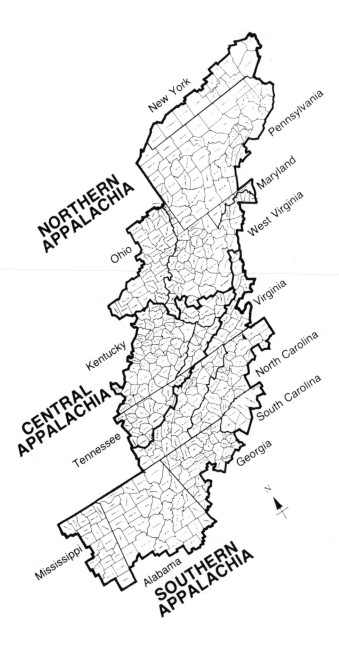

Map 5-1. The Appalachian Region.

cochairman prior to formal meetings. The staff has tended to favor people-oriented social service programs and facilities, concentrations of funding, and innovative approaches.[1] Not content with the veto power exercised by their regional representative, the states have recently sought to increase their influence over the choice of projects by forming a state management committee composed of states' staff to consider items on the commission agenda and to make recommendations independent of the commission staff (Figure 5-1).

At the state level, the governors' state representatives usually double as the directors of their respective state offices of economic development or planning. Moreover, all states have designated an official to handle Appalachian program activities, although the arrangement differs from state to state and depends largely on the relative importance of the Appalachian program in state affairs. West Virginia, the only state wholly included in Appalachia, for example, has an Appalachian development office in its office of federal/state relations. In contrast, the Appalachian program in New York or Ohio is only one relatively minor responsibility of the state planning office or office of community and economic development. The multi-county local development districts discussed earlier are the creations of state laws or executive orders. They are the last, and perhaps the weakest, link in the Appalachian Regional Commission's planning chain.

The Appalachian Regional Development Act of 1965 did not require that a single regional investment plan be formulated. In contrast to the Economic Development Act's (Title V) commissions' regional plans, the decision was made early in the Appalachian Regional Commission's development to have individual state plans for their Appalachian areas in lieu of a single regionwide plan formulated by the commission and staff. Thus, the commission evolved a state-by-state approach to projects and funding, and the commission was given responsibilities for providing research, analysis, and recommendations to the states.

Budgets and Funding

The Appalachian Regional Commission is authorized to spend federal funds on a highway program, grant-in-aid programs (including health care demonstration projects, land restoration, vocational education,

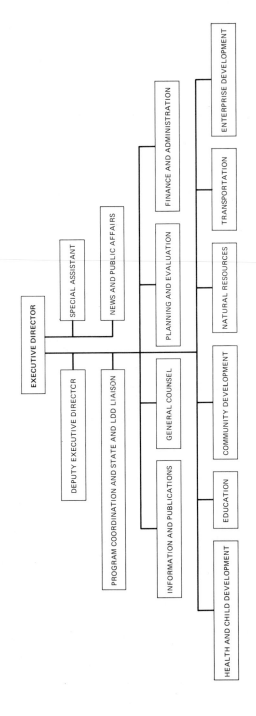

Figure 5-1. Appalachian Regional Commission Organization.

and a variety of supplemental grants), housing, research and a catch-all of other support for local development districts. With the exception of the latter two programs, none is fully operated by the commission. Although the commission sets the allocation formulas for states' participation in all its programs, the funds are appropriated to the President who transfers them to the federal cochairman who, in turn, transfers the funds to the federal agencies involved with the commission in the projects. The supplemental grant program (Section 214) allows commission funds to be used to increase the federal portion of existing grant-in-aid programs to 80 percent. Other Appalachian efforts either supplement existing federal efforts or fund demonstration projects.

This incomplete control over program funds was won from the individual federal agencies in 1967 over the objections of the Bureau of the Budget (now the Office of Management and Budget), which has made a determined effort to keep the Appalachian Regional Commission from becoming an operating agency. Between 1967 and 1971, authorizations were earmarked for each category of program, but since then a single appropriation has been made for other than highway programs leaving it to the commission to formulate and justify priorities and allocations.[2]

Until 1975, the allocation programs developed by the commission established accounts for each state by program. State projects could be funded from their share according to the state plans. Criteria included population and geographic size as well as a relevant indication of need—for example, number of high school age youths not enrolled in school for the vocational education projects. Highway funds were expended according to priorities established to bring segments of the system up to uniform adequacy.

Beginning in 1975, the nonhighway allocation mechanism was changed as a result of congressional and commission concern about the differing intensity of need among Appalachian subregions. Each state now receives a basic amount for nonhighway programs, excluding research and local development district support—80 percent of the fiscal year 1974 level (or $82.4 million in fiscal 1975)—and a subregional amount based on per capita income levels. States with areas in more than one subregion receive separate allocations for each. The main beneficiary is central Appalachia; the $38.6 million for fiscal 1975 amounted to $5.14 per person in central Appalachia compared to $1.47 for the northern, and $2.29 for the southern subregion.[3] Another $2 million was set aside for conservation and recreation projects in the highlands areas of Appalachia, which overlay the north, central, and southern regions, and $8.5 million for research and support of the development districts.

The administrative budget of the commission is shared equally by the federal government and the states, who contribute according to an allocation formula. In fiscal 1975 both contributed almost $1.5 million to operate the Commission. In addition, the federal government expended $0.3 million to support the federal cochairman and his staff.

Assuming that the types of aid funded under the Area Redevelopment Act and its successor, the Economic Development Act, would be available in Appalachia, the drafters of the Appalachian Regional Development Act produced a broader set of programs to suit the region's development needs. In terms of federal dollars committed, the highway construction program is the Appalachian Regional Commission's most notable undertaking. However, the commission's mandates to improve the health, education, housing, and environmental standards for Appalachians have allowed the federal government to experiment with programs focused on building the social base necessary before economic expansion can occur. The regional commission, the local development districts, and the funds were to be levers to pry open federal doors to enable Appalachians to share fully in federal programs requiring state or local contributions. When other federal, state, and local funds are considered, the nonhighway program expenditures exceed those of the highway program (Figure 5-2).

Leveraging was the way of making up for the financial inadequacies of local governments and of encouraging local interest in health, child development, education, and vocational training. Monies to raise the local share for building facilities and to help plan and operate programs were made available. The other necessary ingredients were grantsmanship to be provided by the local development districts and the ombudsman in Washington—the commission and its staff. This unique combination of devices has allowed the commission to promote many experiments in delivering social development services in Appalachia.

Transportation

One of the major areas in which the Appalachian Regional Commission's founders believed the region had much catching up to do

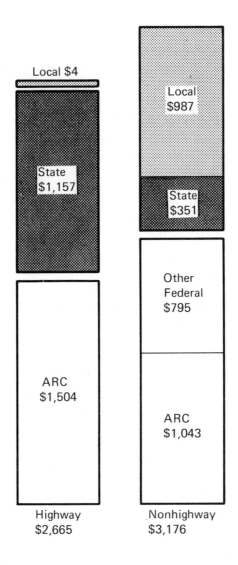

Source: Appalachian Regional Commission, *1975 Annual Report to the Appalachian Regional Commission* (Washington: The Commission, 1974), Table 7.

Figure 5-2. Sources of Funds for Appalachian Programs, Fiscal 1966-1975 (Millions).

was in roadbuilding. The President's Appalachian Regional Commission (PARC) asserted that "(d)evelopment activity in Appalachia cannot proceed until the regional isolation has been overcome."[4] The commission proposed, and Congress accepted, an initial six-year program of construction costing $1.2 billion in federal funds to pave 2,100 miles of highways. Five hundred miles of access roads were also planned—to be built in less than five-mile stretches, serving recreational, industrial, and residential facilities. The program has undergone several expansions and in mid-1975 called for $2.1 billion in federal funds to be used to extend the system to 2,700 miles of highways and 1,500 miles of access roads by 1978. As it turned out, the promised funds had little relation to reality and will be adequate to cover only part of the ambitious road construction plan.

A Direction for the Highway Program

The PARC outlined broadly the goals of the highway program: to penetrate the poorly served areas of the region and to provide linkages between interstate highways. In contrast with the usual approach to roadbuilding, the goal was to generate demand, not to follow existing development. Initially the Appalachian Regional Commission set more specific aims: to attain on the newly-built highways an average speed of 50 miles per hour and a capability of carrying traffic adequate for projected 1990 levels. Each state rated the adequacy of the roads in proposed Appalachian corridors, and a "worst first" priority system was accepted. Each state received an annual allocation of funds proportional to the costs of its share of the proposed highways.

While the regular federal roadbuilding program called for a 50 percent federal share, the Appalachia law allowed a federal share of up to 70 percent of the costs of the highways if the commission determined that construction could not proceed without added help. The extra 20 percent was based on the belief that the strained fiscal capacity of Appalachian states might call for more federal help than other areas receive to get the system built. However, since gasoline taxes are earmarked exclusively for highway construction, observers have questioned whether the Appalachian states had deferred highway investment due to tight budgets.[5]

The fiscal capacity question was overridden by a more important consideration: the PARC and Congress had estimated a lower price tag than was realistic for the highway system. The Appalachian Regional Commission, therefore, decided that to build as many miles as possible per federal dollar, the state and local match would have to be 50 percent. Only in 1974, after the federal share in other highway programs was raised to 70 percent, did the commission agree to raise its contribution.

Critics have claimed that Appalachia already had its fair share of rural highway mileage before the Act was passed.[6] Nevertheless, commission advocates argue that existing roads were inefficient and poorly planned, and Appalachian states persist in the belief that highways are a top priority. In 1971 the total U.S. state and local government direct expenditure on highways accounted for 12 percent of their total budgets. With three exceptions, in the Appalachian states, the proportion was higher. In Pennsylvania, Kentucky, West Virginia, and Tennessee, which account for six of ten eligible Appalachian miles, the comparable percentages invested in highways ranged from 14 to 28 percent.[7]

Results

The heavy federal investment in additional highways for Appalachia and its probable impact on state and local priorities must be justified on the ground that highways could provide the area with benefits other programs could not. Transportation is an important factor in industrial location, and a 1969 Appalachian Regional Commission study showed that over 60 percent of new firms that moved into Appalachia between 1965 and 1968 located within twenty minutes of a new highway. During the first six years of the program, there were no commission funds available to promote industrial development because a legislative ban on aid to private businesses was interpreted to preclude industrial site development as well. Beginning in fiscal 1972 the commission began a very modest $1 million a year program to allow states the chance to further influence development. Initially, most of the funds were to be used to plan the types of development the particular states prefer to attract.[8] The next logical step would be for states and development districts to apply for site preparation funds; the Economic Development Administration might be one source of funds for this purpose. It is too early to assess the results of this approach.

The Appalachian Regional Commission has not quantified the gains in access to public services accruing to the highway program.

Assuming a direct relationship between access and growth centers, and taking into account that the lion's share of the commission's public facilities investments are associated with growth centers, the public services and highway aspects of the Appalachian program are probably complementary.

Critics of the highway emphasis in the Appalachian program have called attention to the problem that the distribution of benefits within the region and its periphery may not live up to expectations. One study has argued that the highway system will enhance the economic potential of urban areas along the perimeter of the region even more than that within Appalachia.[9] These predictions still point to better economic lives for the Appalachian people, although place-oriented benefits may fall disproportionately outside the region's boundaries.

Costs

The most widespread criticism of the Appalachian highway program has been of its climbing costs. In 1970, after only five years of the program, the General Accounting Office estimated that the costs had risen from $1.2 billion to $3.85 billion.[10] As previously mentioned, the commission realized from the outset that the costs of the planned corridors had been underestimated. But aside from inflation and the customary cost overruns, other factors contributed to the rising price tag: improved safety standards, new requirements to aid displaced persons, added mileage, and the upgrading of some two-lane to four-lane roads also raised costs.

Although Congress has increased the authorizations to $2.1 billion and the commission has followed a conservative policy of matching on a 50/50 basis, inflation alone since 1970 added another 35 percent to the costs by mid-1975. Moreover, as the 70/30 matching policy has been adopted, the federal dollar will build fewer miles.

In many areas of Appalachia the terrain contributes to higher costs per mile than the nationwide norm. But other reasons may also contribute to the wide differentials in costs. In 1972 the average interstate highway cost $1.8 million per mile to build, compared to between $5 and $6 million per Appalachian mile.[11]

Regionalism

On paper the highway system serves regional goals linking interstate routes and crossing state lines. Nevertheless in over a decade of implementation, the planned spans have been completed by individual states according to the commission's priority rating scheme—the most badly needed improvements first. The commission has defended its handling of the program contending that it would be inefficient to overlay new organizations and procedures on the regular federal/state highway mechanism and that the commission was not designed to divest governors of decision-making authority. The General Accounting Office countered that one purpose of forming a regional commission for Appalachia was to provide an alternative to the piecemeal approaches of the past federal aid programs.[1 2]

A patient Congress has argued little with the states' approach to building the highway system. The commission continues to assure Congress that it is working with the states on their priorities and to warn against prejudging the highway system before it is completed and the full benefits realized. There may be more than ideological championing of state rights to the commission approach, and maximizing state autonomy may have paid off. By not insisting on a regional plan for completing full corridors of highways, Congress has no choice but to appropriate funds annually until completion if a regionwide impact is to be realized and if incomplete highways are to be avoided.

As of the beginning of 1975, 1,038 miles of the development highway system were completed, and 307 miles were under construction; engineering and right-of-way were in progress for another 729 miles. On only some 625 miles, then, of authorized highway had no action been taken.

Additional Transportation Needs

The completion of the proposed highway system is not likely to serve fully Appalachia's transportation needs. Air travel is essential for a transportation system, and services in Appalachia are inferior. In

1971 the commission received $8.5 million to provide supplemental grants for airport construction safety projects. By the end of fiscal 1975, $17 million had been spent for projects, more than doubling the amount of supplemental grant funds spent on airports. This is part of a slight shift in emphasis away from using most of the commission's supplemental grant funds for health and education facilities.

Another transportation problem is rural public transportation. The commission has helped three local development districts complete studies and prepare proposals for improved bus service in their areas. Support of rural mass transit is catching on in Congress as well. The 1973 Federal-Aid Highway Act sets aside $30 million to be expended on demonstration projects in fiscal 1975 and 1976. A limited number of rural areas and small cities, which have long protested the focus of attention on urban mass transit, will be able to buy buses or build fringe parking or other facilities.

Health and Child Development

Next to highway construction, the Appalachian program emphasized child development and education. The original Appalachian bill earmarked funds to be used for up to 80 percent of the costs of health facilities construction; supplemental grants to increase the federal share of other agencies' health facilities construction up to the same proportion are also available (Table 5-1). The Appalachian Regional Commission can cover total operating costs during the first two years, but the commission's share drops to 75 percent for the succeeding three years before aid is terminated. The commission is also authorized to provide up to 75 percent of health planning projects. Since 1969 the Appalachian child development program has supplemented other federal programs for these services. The commission spent $63 million for health and child development programs in 1975 divided as follows:

	(millions)
Child development operations	$23
Health program operations	21
Health facilities construction	14
Health planning	3

Table 5-1
Appalachian Regional Commission Supplemental Grants, Fiscal 1966-1975

Type of Project	Number of Projects	Amount (millions)
Total	2,142	$383
Education	807	143
Vocational education	482	73
Higher education	230	56
National Defense Education Act	67	7
Water, sewer and sewage treatment	521	106
Health facilities	418	88
Libraries	122	12
Airports	136	17
Other	138	17

Source: *1975 Annual Report of the Appalachian Regional Commission* (Washington: The Commission, 1976), in press.

Of the total, $53 million came from the state block grant allocations, $8 million was earmarked by the health section of the Act and the balance was in the form of supplemental grants for building health facilities.

Building institutions and capabilities in planning and operating health programs is a major policy goal of the Appalachian Regional Commission. Construction of facilities, which accounted for 60 percent of the $74 million spent on health programs during the commission's first five years, has declined in importance. Since 1968, 12 health demonstration areas have been outlined, and within these multicounty districts advisory councils of local professionals, public officials, and lay persons plan and operate community health service programs. The commission requires the states to offer a broad range of health services in the demonstration areas, and a 1974 survey by the commission reported that 76 percent of the projects did screening, diagnosis, and treatment. A third were involved in out-reach and public education; a wide range of home care, emergency, speech and hearing, and other options were being followed. In 1971 communities outside the demonstration areas became eligible for planning funds and for funds to operate centers serving only the day-to-day health needs of the residents, but able to refer patients for more extensive and specialized treatment. These "extender" facilities have allowed some areas to make up for the shortage of accredited medical personnel with paraprofessionals who work with physicians.

The development of state and local institutions to plan and organize projects is an important element of the child development program. The commission required the states to establish interagency councils representing state efforts focusing on the needs of children, including day care, maternal health, nutrition, and social services. In some states the policies set by these councils are carried out by multicounty groups, and in others line agencies in the counties administer the projects. In either case, multicounty local development districts or local child development councils attempt to coordinate the program across counties. As a result, not all child development projects can operate from a single day care center, providing medical, educational and nutritional services, and many must depend on referral to the traditional agencies specializing in social services at the county level.

Assessing Health and Child Development

There can be no doubt that the Appalachian Regional Commission has been responsible for introducing many new health and child development services to the region. All but eight Appalachian counties are involved in comprehensive health planning, 70 primary health care centers have opened, and the 233 child development projects served 103,000 families and children during fiscal 1974. In fact, several of Appalachia's demonstration projects may have had a payoff outside the region. The primary health care program served as a model for rural health programs of the Robert Wood Johnson Foundation. The child development projects have been called a "national laboratory," serving a broader range of clientele than welfare mothers.

The projects have also generated employment. A fiscal 1974 survey estimated that 9,000 jobs were created, including many slots for mothers of day care enrollees and for paramedical personnel. And, while it is impossible to measure how many employee-hours and how much in wages could accrue due to improved health care, the commission cited several instances of industries locating close to hospitals built or saved with the help of commission funds.

Like all Appalachian programs, the demonstration projects were undertaken with the hope that they eventually would operate independently, but viability is a critical issue. In 1974 the commission found that two-thirds of the health projects were still operating. Considering the statutory five-year cutoff of commission support, all those responding thought they could continue. The anticipated sources of funds were largely fees and service contracts combined with a variety of state, local, and private contributions. In contrast to the health projects, the major non-commission sources of child development aid are other federal grants. In 1974 the commission provided half the funds, Title IV-A of the Social Security Act another 39 percent, and other federal programs 4 percent; the state and local share was only 7 percent. The child development programs, then, without a much more substantial state and local commitment, will remain creatures of the federal budget and probably could not survive the loss of commission funds.

Education Projects

Like the Appalachian Regional Commission's health program, the education program emphasized initially the construction of facilities. And until 1971 the law provided only for the construction and equipment of vocational facilities. Measured in dollars, the bulk of 1974 vocational education program was bricks and mortar:

Construction and equipment	$20 million
Operations	3 million
Demonstration and administration	2 million

More recently, improvements in the content of education, the quality of personnel, and regional cooperative efforts have been given greater priority. The 1971 amendments authorized payment for demonstration projects, paralleling those of the health program, to cover up to 75 percent of planning expenses, and 100 percent for the first two years and 75 percent for the following three for operating expenses.

The policy established by the commission at its outset was to enroll at least half of the region's high school juniors and seniors in vocational curricula. The commission estimated that 150 schools operated by the fall of 1975 with an enrollment of close to 300,000 students.[13] If this estimate is verified and sustained, then the commission will have met its goal of providing vocational education to half the 11th and 12th graders.

The use of supplemental funds to help build higher education facilities is likely to be discouraged in the coming years since the commission has found a surfeit of excess space in higher education classrooms. A combination of factors accounted for the over-building, including the commission's lack of good data and the failure of states to foresee the slowed growth in enrollments. A quantity versus quality problem also arises. Although there is extra space and although higher education institutions in Appalachia are producing proportionally more teachers than appear to be needed due to lower birth rates, many Appalachian facilities are old and many Appalachian teachers underqualified. The commission must encourage the states to be more selective in their investments in higher education, replacing outdated facilities and upgrading the existing teaching staff.

The commission favored demonstration projects for all levels of education, but until 1975 Congress qualified only aid for vocational education. Nevertheless, the commission was able to allocate other research and demonstration funds for planning and operating multi-county regional education service agencies (RESA). Among the twenty-one agencies operating in 1974 the most common activities were conducting staff development courses, providing centralized library or audio-visual equipment, group purchasing of supplies, and several special education programs. The existence of these education agencies also helped Appalachia share in a space-age demonstration program funded by Health, Education and Welfare and the National Aeronautics and Space Administration, which broadcast education programs from the University of Kentucky to teachers in five RESAs. Pooling resources is one of the major goals in creating these institutions. Local resources, which provide over half of school district expenditures nationwide, account for less than 30 percent in areas served by the commission-assisted agencies.

Appalachian educational deficiencies remain, although adequate facilities appear to exist. Dropout and illiteracy rates exceed the national norms. Localities have difficulty raising funds for school expenditures. While states and federal sources take up some of the slack, per capita revenues fall short of those nationwide. If doctors and dentists could be convinced to stay in Appalachia after graduation, their education would provide a payoff to the people in the region. Over 140 Appalachian counties have critical medical shortages, and more than 120 face severe shortages of dentists.[14]

Although the commission will likely broaden its education programs beyond vocational training, it admittedly can have only a small direct impact on Appalachian education. The commission estimates that its dollars account for only 1 percent of all education expenditures in Appalachia. Any real impact must come from the joint ventures and shared experiences of local school districts and the states. And, as is true with the child development demonstration projects, the viability of multicounty education agencies will depend heavily on continued federal and state support.

Housing and Community Development

Appalachia's housing deficiencies were documented by the President's Appalachian Regional Commission—the federal government classified over a quarter of its dwelling units in 1960 as dilapidated or deteriorating, compared with less than a fifth nationwide. There was no housing provision, however, in the original Act. Two years later the commission lobbied successfully to add a revolving loan fund for Appalachian states to help provide up to 80 percent of the costs incurred in applying for federal housing aid and a technical assistance program to promote state housing finance agencies. In 1971 grants for site development were added to the authorizations.

Although the funds available are meager—about $1 million annually, not counting a special $1.5 million effort in fiscal 1973 for Hurricane Agnes repairs—some advances have been made. As of 1974, 11 of the 13 Appalachian states had created state housing agencies; nine had help from the commission.[15] This is the type of permanent institution building that the commission has tried to stimulate in all its programs. By the end of 1974 about half of the 12,000 units planned with the help of over 100 "seed money" planning loans were completed. ARC takes pride in this achievement since only 600 low and moderate income housing units were built in the region between 1961 and 1967 under federal housing programs.[16] But some credit also must go to the Great Society's initiatives and implementations during the first Nixon administration, under which the federal government subsidized four times as many housing units in 1974 as a decade earlier.

Complementing the housing program, water and sewer grants represent a growing share of the supplemental grant program as education projects receive less emphasis. Water and sewer projects accounted for a fourth of the funds distributed for supplemental grants between 1966 and 1974. Although in some cases service has been extended to industrial sites, the improvement of health and living standards, not job creation, is the major goal.

Natural Resources

Despite the many specific proposals advanced prior to the Appalachian Regional Commission Act, the resulting legislation was short on natural resource funds. The for-profit timber development organizations proposed were dropped by Congress in favor of planning organizations and an added provision to use existing Department of Agriculture loan funds. The commission thought the planning groups unworkable, and dropped the program after one year. The Army Corps of Engineers spent $5 million between 1966 and 1970 on a water resources survey that resulted in several recommendations, but little construction. Land stabilization contracts between farmers and the Department of Agriculture's efforts to restore soil and to prevent erosion went unfunded after 1970; some $19 million was spent in earlier years. Only the mine restoration program administered by the Department of the Interior's Bureau of Mines has survived the first decade of operations.

The mine restoration program allows the Bureau of Mines to contract for the planning and engineering of sealing abandoned mines, extinguishing mine fires, reclaiming surface land, and abating water pollution from mine drainage. The commission furnishes the only source of funds to act on acid drainage problems; other federal agencies provide research funds. Much of the funding of mine restoration programs is carried over from year to year as the Bureau of Mines is slow in completing its contract process. In fiscal 1974 $4 million was authorized. The 1975 Senate report on the Appalachian Regional Development Act amendments chastised the Bureau of Mines for the delays and recommended a provision allowing public or nonprofit bodies to indemnify the federal government for losses resulting from claims against the projects.[17]

Responding to the increased demand for coal resources as oil prices were raised, the commission has launched a series of energy studies. Beginning in 1975, research has been planned on the technology of coal conversion, energy supply and demand, and environmental concerns. An important result could be a realistic assessment of the contribution increased coal demand will have on the economy of the region.

Appalachia and Regionalism

The emphasis on Appalachian multistate regionalism was to be found mostly in the rhetoric of its proponents, but little in the operations of the Appalachian Regional Commission. With the exception of the highway program, other Appalachian efforts are based on state planning for local projects. Deferring to the state "partners," the commission allowed the states flexibility in spending nonhighway funds, postponing regional health, education or natural resource projects to some future date.

Moreover, the variation and contrast in sources of economic distress has produced a reevaluation of the homogeneity of Appalachian needs. Since 1970 the four subregions have been given separate recognition, and beginning with fiscal 1975 states spent a portion of their funds according to subregion priorities. In the north, investment to renew the aging infrastructure was the listed priority.[18] The southern areas used their investments to promote rural/urban balance, diversify employment, emphasize investment in growth areas, and develop community leadership. So-called enterprise development—water and sewer projects, housing and recreational facilities—were to be the first order of business. As with other attempts to find a workable means of setting local development priorities, the substate strategy results in goals that are broad enough to justify most any commission investment. Although the commission claims to take subregional goals into account in approving projects, it is clear that the states prefer to maintain as much discretion as they can in expending funds.

Public Works: Foundations for Growth

The federal government is a major contributor to the country's economic infrastructure. In fiscal 1974 federal support for public works construction was estimated at more than $13 billion.[1] Direct federal construction accounted for less than four-tenths of the total—$3.3 billion for civil and $1.7 billion for defense projects. Most assistance took the form of grants in aid—approximately $8.1 billion in fiscal 1974—and over half of the grant funds were expended for highways.

The extent to which federal public works programs influence economic development is a matter of degree and perspective. A 1970 survey of federal programs with possible impact on the pattern of economic development concluded that public facilities are necessary to sustain development, but do not stimulate the process initially.[2] This study and others observed that with the possible exception of highway programs, federal aid is addressed to current, not future, needs. The authors of the study conclude that highway expenditures have had the greatest impact on economic development, and that influence has been biased toward urban areas.[3]

Within the perspective of the total size and potential influence of public works on economic development, those programs aimed specifically at alleviating long-run economic distress are small indeed. In fiscal 1974 the Economic Development Administration and the Appalachian Regional Commission expended about $400 million for public works, or less than 5 percent of all federal public works outlays. These efforts cannot be anticipated, then, to have a noticeable economy-wide impact. It is their influence on local economies by which they must be judged.

The Economic Development Administration and Public Works

The foundations of the Area Redevelopment Act were laid in the belief that the lack of venture capital was at the root of the problems of depressed areas. But by the time the economic development legislation was rewritten in 1965, public works had gained greater political support. President Johnson's request called for a $250 million public works authorization for the Economic Development Administration in 1965, the Senate raised the ante to $400 million, and the House to $500 million, which was the initial authorization.

Legislative Standards

To qualify for public works grants and loans, applicants must be units of government, Indian tribes, or nonprofit organizations. Three broad types of projects can be funded. The first is land acquisition or development—such as industrial site preparation. Improvements for public works, public service or development facility usage are a second category; they most often take the form of water and sewer hookups for industrial parks or needy residential areas. The final classification includes acquisition, construction, rehabilitation, alteration, expansion or improvement of facilities and covers a wide variety of projects from the building of swimming pools and community centers on Indian reservations to the renovation of aging warehouses and industrial buildings for an industrial park in an urban renewal area.

Banned from Economic Development Act assistance are projects leading to the production of goods and services for which there is insufficient demand or for which existing capacity is adequate to produce the additional supply. In practice capacity studies are rarely done, although in the case of Indian tribal businesses, for example, they have been useful in discouraging unrealistic enterprises. Advance information about prospective firms that would be attracted by public works projects are normally not available. When a study is requested, the regional office representatives who negotiate and process applications for public works are responsible for asking that it be done. Given the state of the art of forecasting the feasibility of new enterprises, it is improbable that this well-intentioned mandate adds much to economic development guidelines.

Project costs are usually shared between the Economic Development Administration and the applicant although the agency is authorized to fund supplemental grants to help designated areas take advantage of other federal programs. However, comingling of funds with the Appalachian Regional Commission was banned—a prohibition dropped in the 1975 amendments to economic development legislation. In the bulk of the cases the cost sharing is equally divided between the Economic Development Administration and the applicant, but there are exceptions. Projects on Indian reservations, in areas with high poverty or unemployment and in jurisdictions that have exhausted their taxing and borrowing authorities can be fully federally funded. Areas designated under the Disaster Relief Act and special impact areas qualify for up to 80 percent federal participation (Table 6-1). Finally, a 10 percent bonus in the maximum grant rate is given to projects in economic development districts.

Economic Development Act loans for public works have been used to supplement grants where communities were unable to raise the local share of a project. The limit is forty years depending on the life expectancy of the project. Interest rates are normally set at the operative U.S. Treasury rate although the Economic Development Administration has the option of setting its rate one-half of a percent lower. The provisions for 100 percent grant rates on Indian reservations and in special impact areas have obviated the need for many loans. In fiscal 1974 only $224,000 of the $174 million in public works funds was obligated for loans.

To secure approval, evidence must be presented indicating that the project would directly or indirectly improve the opportunities for expanding or establishing industry in the area, that it will create long-term job opportunities in the future, or that it provides a needed service to the chronically unemployed or the poor in the community. An approved overall economic development plan also is required.

Table 6-1
Need and Maximum Public Works Grant Rates under the Economic Development Act

Maximum Grant as Percent of Cost	Criteria
80	1. Median family income less than $3,500, or 2. Unemployment rate 12 percent or higher.
70	1. Median family income $3,501 to $4,000, or 2. Unemployment rate 10 to 11.9 percent.
60	1. Median family income $4,001 to $4,500, or 2. Unemployment rate 8 to 9.9 percent.

An exception to the goals of stimulating long-term economic growth was added in the 1971 amendments. Special impact areas (designed as needy on the basis of a large concentration of poverty, substantial unemployment, an actual or threatened abrupt rise in unemployment, or heavy outmigration in rural areas) could apply for public works grants that would give immediate and useful work to the area's needy. Reacting to the 1971 recession, Congress provided that between 25 and 35 percent of public works funds be spent for the Public Works Impact Program (PWIP). In 1973 Congress refused an administration request to kill the program, but did lower the minimum PWIP investment to 10 percent of the public works budget.

Project Administration

Congress placed a few constraints on the public works program. In fact, given the broad eligibility and standards for accepting projects, the Economic Development Administration has been a popular source of funds. The approval of projects that were long in getting off the ground was an early problem, and agency efforts to increase efficiency were not always successful.

One of every nine public works projects obligated between 1966 and 1969 was not underway in 1970. The House Public Works Committee scrutinized the problems faced by the delayed projects.[4] It found that the difficulties were much the same as those that the Area Redevelopment Administration had experienced during its first two years when it was able to disburse barely a tenth of its obligated public works funds. Two examples of the underlying causes were the failure of a bond issue to raise the local share and the inability of communities to recruit enough users for a new water system to ensure loan repayment. Compounding any delay was the provision that if obligated funds were not used by the end of the fiscal year, they could not be shifted to another project. It was either the obligated projects or nothing, and the agency chose nursing possible projects along over returning funds to the Treasury.

Burdened by the large pool of pending projects and frequent rejections, the Economic Development Administration took steps in 1969 to avoid the embarrassment of rejecting applications. The agency succeeded in reducing rejections by arranging for advance conferences with potential applicants allowing regional officials to weed out projects that are not likely to get a positive recommendation from the regional director or final approval in Washington. Agency officials indicated that the time invested in meeting with applicants, especially on their first proposal, presented an invaluable opportunity to go over the legal and technical aspects of the grants and to discourage formal applications for projects that could not pass muster.

Careful screening of projects also may help reduce the likelihood of delays in their completion, but considerable time will still be required after approval before construction begins. As of the end of fiscal 1974, data from 1,565 finished public works projects showed that they averaged 44 weeks from approval to the start of construction and another 73 weeks to completion.[5]

Following the pattern of most federal agencies since 1969, the Economic Development Administration has decentralized preapplication procedures, project monitoring, and the authorization to approve small changes in grants to its regional offices. Final grant approval, however, remains in the hands of the assistant secretary in Washington. The Washington office is responsible for fiscal evaluation and policy setting, but central monitoring is confined to projects that the regional office flags for problems.

An Assessment

Through the multiplier effect, government expenditures can be expected to raise the output of a region, improving incomes and employment, encouraging inmigration, and contributing to local ability to finance public services. However, to separate the impact of relatively small efforts, such as the public works investments of the Economic Development Administration or the Appalachian Regional Commission, from the rest and account for them in terms of regional improvements in socioeconomic indicators is difficult to manage. And for any such analysis, decades will have to elapse before it is feasible to measure the total impact of investments in public works. The life expectancy of water and sewer systems or industrial parks may be as great as forty years, and the oldest public works projects are only fifteen years old. An acceptable approach to the evaluation of public works for economic development must be, first, on a project-by-project basis. But it also should go beyond benefit-cost analysis to examine if the types of projects undertaken fit the goals of economic development policy.

The Economic Development Administration's Evaluation Design

The Economic Development Administration's methodology for evaluating its public works program was established in 1969.[6] It reflects a policy that job creation is the most important aspect of public works. The evaluation procedures were applied to 274 projects in 1970, which represented over 80 percent of those projects more than a year old.[7] A reevaluation of 50 of those projects in 1974 applied the same methodology.[8]

Following the mandate of the legislation, the evaluation attempted to measure the project's impact on the creation of job opportunities, contributions to a stable and diversified economy, provision of needed services, and influence on the community's economic development activities. The job creation impact included a count of positions created or saved due to the project and an estimate of the multiplier effect of the new employment in the community. Direct jobs were counted and the payroll divided by the average manufacturing wage to compute direct job equivalents. Because in larger areas a greater proportion of the labor force is employed in serving local residents, it was assumed that each direct job created generated 0.4 indirect jobs in communities of 5,000 to 10,000—the typical size area for projects—0.7 in those between 25,000 and 100,000, and 1.3 in cities of over 1 million. Estimates of possible future jobs were based on the expansion plans of the businesses benefiting from the project. The Economic Development Administration investment for each indirect job and combination of direct and indirect job equivalents was calculated. Finally, a description of the firm's size, capital investment, product, and reasons for locating were considered.

Measurements of job creation lend themselves more easily to quantification than the other three criteria, which are more subjective. Improvements in the structure of the local economy were "graded." The factors considered included the number of new employees or those whose jobs were "saved" for residents of the designated area, the number who were heads of households, and the rise in income, which gave the greatest weight to the employment of idle workers whose earnings were presumably zero. The evaluation also considered whether or not the firm represented a new industry for the area and belonged to a stable parent company. The project's service contribution was rated according to whether the service was new, improved, or marginal and whether the poor and minority residents benefited, the highest grade going to projects providing a significant new service to a substantial number of low-income residents. Changes in the economic development process in the area were measured by opinions of community leaders on new attitudes and activities regarding economic development and the Economic Development Administration's influence on these changes.

The Economic Development Administration's evaluation design, like those of all federal agencies, reflects the art of the possible. While data on jobs created in connection with the project are the most easily collected, the attribution of jobs to agency funding is more subjective. The count of indirect jobs, although based on empirical research, must be taken on faith, and no distinction is made between jobs created in the public and private sectors. Computation of job equivalents, as opposed to direct jobs, gives more credit if higher than average-paying jobs result. The comparison is useful for studying the quality of the jobs, while the direct job count identifies the number of individuals benefiting from the project.

Job Creation: The Major Goal

As the public works program got underway in 1966, an emphasis on water and sewer projects and industrial parks carried over from the Area Redevelopment Act's Accelerated Public Works Program. A bias in favor of projects linked directly to expanding business opportunities in the area also has remained. Between fiscal 1966 and 1975, half of the obligated public works projects were for general industrial and commercial development facilities, mostly water and sewer projects, and one of every five projects involved industrial park and site development (Table 6-2).

Table 6-2
Economic Development Administration Public Works Projects, 1966 to 1975

Type of Project	Number	EDA Investment (millions)
Total	3,746	$1,759
General industrial/commercial development facilities	1,861	819
Industrial park, site development	793	331
Recreation and tourism	279	154
Educational facilities	151	98
Port and harbor facilities	106	122
Airport facilities	55	29
Health facilities	89	64
Other public facilities	412	142

Source: U.S. Department of Commerce, *1975 Annual Report, Economic Development Administration* (Washington: Government Printing Office, 1975), in press.

Water and Sewer Projects; Industrial Parks

Projects to build or upgrade water and sewage treatment facilities are relatively inexpensive from the Economic Development Administration's standpoint and are the most frequently funded type of community or industrial and commercial facility built with agency funds. The average cost of water and sewer projects during the agency's first decade was about $300,000. A random sampling of these water and sewer projects might include an $81,900 grant to help extend water and develop sewer facilities to an industrial park in Centralia, Illinois, built with the help of a local businessmen's organization; a $25,000 grant coupled with a $25,000 loan to extend the Louisa, Kentucky, water supply to a previously unserved part of town containing residences, some industries, a hospital, and nursing home; and a $56,000 grant to Peever, South Dakota, on the Sisseton-Wahpeton Indian Reservation for a sewage treatment plant and collection system serving the town and a Bureau of Indian Affairs school to be built there shortly afterwards.

Water and sewer projects often supplement industrial park projects. For example, Johnson County, Kentucky, was the beneficiary of a $773,000 grant to develop an industrial park and to extend the water system from the city of Paintsville out to the park. Industrial site preparation might also involve grading, drainage, canal dredging, or the building of access roads. A combination of two or more forms of assistance is the basis for the agency's definition of an industrial park project.

Although Economic Development Administration studies suggested that 100 to 150 acre industrial parks were the most cost effective, a sample of 53 parks (not including those on Indian reservations) indicated that many were less than 60 acres and were located in communities with a median population of 8,500.[9] Most of the areas helped were relatively isolated from heavily populated areas. The average firm locating in these parks employed just over 100 persons in 1974. Of the nineteen industrial parks located on Indian reservations, which were surveyed simultaneously, eleven had 50 developed acres or less and twelve were located where the reservation population was under 5,000. Largely due to the vast size of western counties, even those located in a metropolitan area or adjoining county were frequently far from heavily populated areas.

Low rates of utilization among non-Indian industrial parks—35 percent in 1971 rising to 50 percent in 1974—have plagued many of the projects, and a 1974 survey concluded that isolation was a contributing factor.[10] The situation on Indian reservations was even more dismal; only 16 percent of developed acreage was occupied in 1974. The survey showed, however, that the small parks were able to use almost all space by attracting just a few tenants, but those with more than 300 developed acres had the most difficult time achieving high levels of utilization.

Other factors tested in the survey included the proximity to a metropolitan area, county population size, and county wage level. No factor was soundly conclusive, and it is obvious that in locating industries the total impact of the several factors must be studied. While population size offers agglomerative economies, low wages in sparsely populated areas might have a countervailing locational pull. The Economic Development Administration's responsibility, then, is the selection of priorities. A "worst first" policy under which smaller areas receive priority must be willing to accept a greater likelihood of limited utilization, other things being equal, or the creation of low-wage, likely unskilled jobs. A policy aimed at growing counties to reduce the risk of failure or low utilization could take advantage of larger markets and would call for bigger parks, but after a point those advantages must be weighed against diseconomies of size and the larger slice of the public works budget required.

Amenities and Education

The agency has funded relatively few projects aimed at enhancing health, educational, or cultural facilities. The few exceptions include libraries, hospitals, community centers, vocational schools, and, in one case, a public television station. The average cost of these projects exceeds the run-of-the-mill public works project and the costs per job are also higher than on the usual projects. For example, the Economic Development Administration's investment per direct and indirect job for an addition to a hospital in Hanover, New Hampshire, was $29,100, but the project may have contributed other nonmeasurable benefits to the community.

Skills centers may be counted among the agency's most innovative projects. Aid can come from two Economic Development Act provisions. Public works grants have helped build the facilities and technical assistance grants have bolstered operating budgets. One outstanding illustration of these projects was a $1.8 million public works grant made in 1972 that enabled the Seattle, Washington, Opportunities Industrialization Center (OIC) to consolidate its classes and expand its enrollment. A $44,000 technical assistance grant two years later contributed to the management of the institution. The OIC's director boasted a 95 percent placement rate and improved relationships with labor unions and the county government.[11]

In many cases, other state and federal aid is important for the success of education projects. Two vocational schools that had received Economic Development Act grants were evaluated for their job creation impact in 1970 and one restudied in 1974. The agency paid half the cost of remodeling and equipping a building in San Diego, California, for use as a skill center at a cost of nearly $3,000 per direct job created. In San Jose the agency supplemented a $2 million Department of Health, Education, and Welfare grant with a $350,000 grant to build and equip a vocational school to serve the low-income school districts in the county. While the investment per job created was approximately $8,000, the much higher total public commitment must be considered. Although it is expensive, the absence of additional support for the operation of the facilities has been blamed for underutilization in less successful training sites.

The type of jobs created must also be examined. Each case study pointed out that the centers were staffed with skilled employees who would not meet the target population criteria. One result is that the calculations of job equivalents would tend to underestimate the investment per job. For example, in San Jose the building of the vocational school generated 45 jobs, but 62 job equivalents at $7,300 a year. The use of job equivalents is more accurately applied in manufacturing where the computation gives extra credit for better-paying positions.

Nevertheless, it is likely that the skills centers have as good, if not better, chances of touching the lives of the target population. Although several have since closed, and some have operated considerably below capacity, the 11 facilities sampled in a 1969-1970 evaluation had a total enrollment of 14,756, of which 10,657 were adult trainees.[12] Half of the total and two-thirds of the adults were unemployed, disadvantaged, or receiving welfare payments prior to enrollment. Participants benefited from income gains in all but one project.

The Economic Development Administration's role in public works projects usually ends when the obligated grant is spent. The operation of the skills centers and their continued contribution to the needy depend on aid from other federal manpower programs administered by Labor, HEW, and the Bureau of Indian Affairs as well as state and local sources. However, the agency's role in providing technical assistance is of continuing importance to facilities such as the San Jose and Central Alabama OICs, an agency to train migratory labor in Missouri or a University of Massachusetts training program for minority business development professionals, which have depended heavily on agency funding.

Tourism and Recreation

Since Area Redevelopment Administration days, public investment in tourism and recreation projects for economic development purposes has been viewed skeptically. The projects proved to be expensive because they were capital-intensive, and the benefits were limited because the jobs created were seasonal, often paying low wages. Nevertheless in many areas long dependent on natural resources, tourism has become a growth industry. This was the case in Rogue River Valley of Oregon where agriculture, canning, lumber, and wood products traditionally provided many of the jobs. During the 1960s parks, ski areas, lakes, and streams began to grow in popularity.

The Economic Development Adminsitration's involvement in the tourism industry there was to provide an $896,000 grant to the city of Ashland to pay half the cost of a 600-seat indoor theater, exhibit hall, and parking lot for the Oregon Shakespearean Festival, which dated back to 1935. The agency was quite proud of its achievements when the project was completed in 1970 and provided 16 new year-round and 19 part-year direct jobs at the festival and additional employment and earnings for businesses dependent on the tourist trade.[13] The project contributed to other impacts on Ashland since the expanded festival has brought more tourists to the area. Private investors renovated their downtown buildings, and several new enterpreneurs located in the area. The local economic development committee has continued to pursue ways to strengthen tourism although public opinion was divided on whether the city should actively promote industrial growth rather than tourism.

Compared to the more common water and sewer or industrial and commercial investments, the Shakespeare Festival was expensive— $25,600 per direct job created compared to less than $2,000 for water and sewer projects or $3,200 for industrial and commercial projects. Other tourism projects covered by Economic Development Administration evaluations, including a convention center and a city park, were comparatively expensive as well. The jobs that the festival project created were administrative, production, and maintenance positions. Most went to Ashland area residents and increased their annual incomes. In addition, although not counted, the theater company was increased by twenty-six members who receive education stipends for their nine or five-month stays. In this instance, the quality of the resulting tourism jobs might be said to be somewhat higher than in most cases although many were not year-round, full-time positions. As would be expected the secondary impact of additional jobs created in stores, motels, and restaurants followed the seasonal and part-time employment pattern.

The Shakespearean Festival was a unique use of Economic Development Act funds and is not typical of public works tourism and recreation projects. State and other parks and resort complexes were more typical. A 1973 review of the tourism and recreation projects found them to be, at their worst, generally costly, creators of seasonal jobs, or unable to contribute substantially to gains in family income.[14] Nevertheless, in many isolated communities with long histories of tourism, investments in convention centers, lodges, and campgrounds may be a desirable development activity.

Such a decision was made by the city officials of North Elba in the Lake Placid area of New York. They decided to build with deficit financing a convention center and ice rink to be free to users.[15] The idea was to stimulate private investment in motels, restaurants, and other aspects of the convention trade. A $480,000 Economic Development Administration grant allowed the project to be completed more quickly and to provide for larger facilities. Few direct jobs have been associated with the investment, although the city reports three new motels, rising land values, and new private investment in the area.

Although the North Elba project has no hopes of making money in the near future, most resorts do. One potential success story is the funding of the Pipestem State Park in southern West Virginia. With the help of a $3.1 million public works grant and a $7.8 million loan, a local nonprofit organization developed a lodge, golf course, an aerial tramway, and other related facilities. The facility opened for business in 1970 and three years later a study found that the project generated 160 jobs at a cost to the Economic Development Administration of about $48,000 per direct job. More employment no doubt has been generated since then. Agency officials feel that Pipestem suggests the potential of concentrated backing. The agency is not in a position, however, to fund many projects of such magnitude.

Urban Public Works

The Economic Development Administration's involvement in metropolitan areas of 250,000 persons or more got off to a poor start in 1966 when an attempt was begun in Oakland to obligate public works funds before the end of the fiscal year and, at the same time, launch an experiment in using economic development funds to cool off a city beset by racial conflict. The largest commitment of funds was in the form of public works. Approximately $23.3 million in grants and $1.6 million in loans was promised initially, and a total of $27.4 million for ten public works projects had been obligated by 1974.[16]

The major recipient of public works funding is the Port of

Oakland—primarily for an airport hangar and support facilities to be leased by World Airways, and a marine terminal, industrial park, and access roads. To ensure that jobs reached minorities and the unemployed, the Economic Development Administration and Oakland officials require lessees and any firm receiving an EDA business loan to submit employment plans and monthly reports on hiring and training. These reports were to be reviewed by a board of businessmen, labor leaders, and minority representatives.

The agency's projects in Oakland faced numerous setbacks. The marine terminal was opposed by the Navy because of concern that the dredging would interfere with plane navigation. Delays in negotiating a lease and employment plan held up the start of the hangar project. Cost overrun estimates followed, which required redesigning the specifications. The failure to meet minority hiring goals required a training project be added. Due to these and other administrative problems, it took six years from the start of Economic Development Administration involvement before the marine terminal was completed in mid-1972. The World Air Center was dedicated the following year. Although the Economic Development Administration's 31-acre portion of the industrial park had attracted only three tenants by 1973, the port expanded the park on its own to 300 acres, and over 180 firms have located there. Finally, the General Accounting Office questioned the agency's generosity with a project that appeared to be able to attract other funds.[17]

On the positive side, EDA's public works projects in Oakland had by 1973 produced their promised jobs.[18] The marine terminal contributed to the volumes of containerized tonnage handled at the Port of Oakland, which is now the second largest container port in the world. But the cost was high—almost $13,000 in public works monies per job—and the delays had soured many within the agency and outside observers on such massive urban commitments. The costs do not reflect the 40 technical assistance grants, which largely supported the public works investments, at a cost of $1.5 million. Only 15 percent of the promised jobs materialized from the five business loans made in Oakland.

Given the size of the annual Economic Development Administration appropriation, the agency could not afford many more commitments the size of Oakland. On that scale, one project would absorb all of the approximately $27 million in public works requested for fiscal 1976 planned for urban projects. Nevertheless, the agency has made several large commitments since Oakland, including the renovation of the Chicago stockyards area, the Brooklyn Navy Yard, and the Harlem Drive (South Bronx) railroad yards. These projects involved the coordination of public works, business development, and technical assistance.

The policy thread connecting the agency's urban public works projects in major metropolitan centers is the rehabilitation of decaying industrial and commercial neighborhoods. The lease guarantee provision added to the business development program in 1974 had the same thrust. However, to change the complexion of large urban centers requires far greater investments than the agency is able to make. While the goal is worthy, the agency cannot mobilize the same type of massive investment, which largely came from local public and private investors, that changed the face of Pittsburgh or Atlanta, for example.

Public Works for Indians

Since its inception, a firm Economic Development Administration policy has been to guarantee a fair share of agency funds for Indian reservations and Alaskan native villages. Some 80 percent of all Indians on reservations and Alaskan natives live in the one hundred fifty-six designated Indian areas. An Indian desk was established at the Washington headquarters to look after Indian interests, and each annual budget has brought a fairly stable commitment of some $20 to $30 million for projects on reservations.

Almost all of the assistance is in the form of public works—industrial parks, community facilities, and infrastructure to support tribal businesses. Business loans to private firms have been rarely used since few private entrepreneurs indicated interest in locating on reservations and because the long processing time has been discouraging.[19] Technical assistance and planning funds have been available as well.

Until fiscal 1974 Indian reservations were subject to the same emphasis as other redevelopment areas to undertake projects that would result directly in jobs and income. Beginning in 1967 sixteen tribes were designated as part of the Selected Indian Reservation Program (SIRP), a joint effort by the Office of Economic Opportunity and the Economic Development Administration to concentrate aid on those reservations with development potential and to work with the Bureau of Indian Affairs and other federal agencies to ameliorate Indian economic deprivation. Five more tribes were added to the list in 1970. The program may have been popular with those reservations getting the most attention, but was not generally well received, and many regional offices gave no priority to the selected few.

The recent change in policy toward Indian needs was not only due to dissatisfaction with SIRP, but more significantly the result of dismal failures with tribally run tourism and recreation projects and with vacant industrial parks built with government funds. One white elephant tourism project was a grant to the Menominee tribal corporation in Wisconsin for a planned visitors' center, museum, campground, motel, and restaurant complex. When a private investor promised to build a 200-room motel and restaurant, the public works project was limited to the visitors' center. The private developer then dropped out, leaving the center to open in 1971 with no overnight facilities to attract tourists to the isolated upper Great Lakes location.[20] Tribal leadership and managerial skills, lacking in this instance and many others, are crucial prerequisites to successful tribal enterprises.

A 1974 survey of nineteen industrial parks on Indian reservations after an average of four years in operation found ten unoccupied.[21] The nine with tenants were only one-third utilized, attracting just twenty-two firms with a total employment of 2,341. Problems included the small labor supply and high turnover rates on many reservations. Among the tenants, Indian-owned firms tended to be undercapitalized and lacking in managerial talent. Branches of stable manufacturing industries had proven difficult to attract.

One of the saddest tales of a successful project turned sour is that of the Fairchild semi-conductor plant in the industrial park at Shiprock, New Mexico. Fairchild benefited from some $3.7 million in Economic Development Act funds spent on the industrial park, water and sewer hookups, and, most importantly, on two business loans to the Navajo tribe. Because any private facility built on the reservation could revert to the tribe at any time, it was up to the tribe to build the plant and lease it to Fairchild. At its height the Fairchild plant was the largest manufacturing firm in New Mexico, had a $4.5 million annual payroll, employed 1,225 persons and received half of the Bureau of Indian Affair's on-the-job training funds. In 1974 following a decline in the demand for its products, heavy layoffs, and a takeover of the plant by dissatisfied employees, Fairchild closed, leaving the Navajo to repay loans on a building for which they have been unable to find a new tenant.

A more heartening example of Indian economic development is the Lummi aquaculture project. Three feasibility studies costing $456,000 and $2.5 million in public works grants have helped the Washington tribe turn their rights to 5,000 acres of tidal pool and the waters of the Nooksack River into a tribal business with oyster and fish hatcheries. Community leadership is one factor to which Economic Development Administration officials contribute much of the project's success. Another important element is the innovative way a traditional source of tribal income, fishing, was converted to a business enterprise. In this case, the capital costs were kept relatively low, and if the 600 jobs materialize, the agency's investment will be approximately $5,000 per job.

However, because the agency must commit a higher proportion of the funds for projects on reservations and is allowed to cover 100 percent of the costs of public works, it often anticipates expensive Indian projects. A $1.5 million tourism and recreation complex on the Fort Berthold reservation was projected to create only 80 jobs, and a $1.8 million one at Blackfeet anticipated just 40 year-round and 125 seasonal openings.[22] Although the cost per acre of reservation industrial parks was lower in the case of the nineteen surveyed in 1974, the cost per job is half again as high as in Economic Development Administration parks off reservations because of the lower levels of utilization of the Indian parks.[23]

During the past several years the agency has adopted policies toward Indian reservations that reflect a more realistic approach to both Indian needs and the Economic Development Administration's capabilities. Community development is the first priority. Multipurpose social centers are well utilized, according to agency officials. And there is the story of the tribe that purchased toilets for every home and held an outhouse bonfire to celebrate a new agency-financed sewer project. The underlying philosophy is first to make reservations viable living places before helping them become attractive places to generate jobs.

Lower priorities are industrial, commercial, and tourism development. Tribal businesses will be steered toward natural resources or goods and services for which demand exists on the reservation. No new industrial parks are planned unless a firm "bird-in-hand" is found. Closer attention is promised to the feasibility of projects, especially large tourism and recreation investments, and the development of sound management skills is to be a critical consideration. The fiscal 1975 budget earmarked no funds for business loans on reservations as the 1974 Indian Financing Act enables the Bureau of Indian Affairs to make loan guarantees, small interest subsidies, and grants for working capital. Since the Economic Development Administration's business loan activity on reservations has been small and generally not a significant factor in the location of private firms on reservations, the programmatic change may not be missed. It would be unwise to reduce options for business assistance to the tribes permanently, however, since many are either ineligible for small business loans or have difficulty raising the necessary collateral.

Issues in Public Works

Who Pays for Economic Growth?

Between fiscal 1966 and 1974 the Economic Development Administration's share in grants and loans for public works projects in which it was the major source of federal funds was just over 60 percent on average (Table 6-3). The agency's share of projects to which supplemental grants were provided was less than 30 percent. These costs did not include the money spent administering the public works program, which in 1971 was estimated as a fourth of the agency's administrative budget.[24] If this proportion still holds, it cost about $5 million in fiscal 1974 to manage the public works program.

Firms locating in the area involved in a public works project normally incur their own capital expenses, but in most instances the portion of the project not covered by an Economic Development Administration grant is raised locally by the city or county and represents additional public investment. Public and private funds spent beyond the scope of the single project, especially in the case of water and sewer, and industrial and commercial projects, also must be counted as costs of economic growth. Water and sewer projects frequently extend to industrial parks built with public funds or in which local investment in utilities has been necessary. Industrial and commercial projects are often supplemented with public expenditures, for example, for streets or access roads to industrial sites or for

Table 6-3

The Economic Development Administration's Share of Public Works Project Costs, 1966-1975 (millions)

Grants and loans	
Total project costs	$2,675
EDA: direct grants	1,397
supplemental grants	134
loans	117
Other funds	1,027
Supplemental to other federal agencies	
Total project costs	$ 393
EDA: supplemental grants	97
loans	13
Other funds: federal	142
nonfederal	141

Source: U.S. Department of Commerce, *1975 Annual Report, Economic Development Administration* (Washington: Government Printing Office, 1976), in press.

complementary facilities in a port development area. In some instances other federal grants are involved. For thirty-one water and sewer projects average public and private capital investment per dollar of EDA investment was:[a]

public	$ 3.01
private	17.11

For ten industrial and commercial projects the ratios were:

public	$ .39
private	3.63

In these thirty-one projects the Economic Development Administration's share of the total capital for economic development was approximately 5 percent. Other public sources contributed 14

[a]U.S. Department of Commerce, Economic Development Administration, *A Comparative Analysis of the Impacts Resulting from 50 Public Works Projects, 1970, 1974*, p. 31. Although the study included thirty-two water and sewer projects, a project involving the extension of a state university at a cost of $55 million public expenditure was deleted from the above computations since it accounted for two-thirds of the other public funds spent on the thirty-two projects.

percent, and the bulk of the capital investment was borne by the private sector—81 percent. These results are not at all surprising because of the emphasis on public works projects that supplement, but do not totally subsidize private enterprise, but it is important to query how significant the federal role is in creating the resulting employment opportunities. If firms can afford the wages, salaries, and over three-quarters of the capital costs of a plant, how significant was the Economic Development Administration's contribution in their decision to locate? Proponents of federal aid argue that the site preparation or upgraded water and sewage treatment facilities can bring needy areas up to competitive standards with other more well-developed locations. On the other hand, it has been argued that the advantages of low-cost labor or access to transportation are at work at the same time, and with or without the Economic Development Administration, the private sector would have found the site anyway.

Job Quality

The jobs associated with Economic Development Act public works projects tend to concentrate in low-wage industries and in low-wage areas.[25] Indeed, the low labor costs in some cases were reported to have been a factor in site selection. In other instances, the jobs created fell short of the average wage because they were part-time, seasonal, or both. Examples are jobs associated with tourism projects, and the new jobs for ticket sellers, vendors, and the like created at one public auditorium and a convention center.

The goal of upgrading target groups can only be a passive one in the long term public works program since the agency can exercise little influence over the private firms locating in industrial parks or using public water and sewer facilities. Data collected on forty-one water and sewer and thirty-one industrial and commercial projects from the public works evaluations funded in 1970-1971 showed that nine of ten jobs went to area residents, six of ten to household heads, and four of nine to the unemployed. However, according to an analysis of fifty-two projects, very few employees had been moved above the poverty level as a result of the jobs.[26]

Since public works jobs depend largely on the decisions of private firms to expand and hire in needy areas, the benefits accruing to the poor and disadvantaged are the result of tightening the local labor market. Because target groups are usually at the end of the labor queue, providing job opportunities will not assure the needy will benefit. Skill training and subsidized on-the-job training are necessary complements to public works if target groups are to be helped compete for skilled jobs.

Long Run Benefits

If public works projects are to play a role in economic or social development, their benefits should be considered beyond the time horizon of a single evaluation year. However, compared to the expected lifespan of most public works undertaken, the experience of economic development programs is limited. Even a project begun in Area Redevelopment Administration days could have, at best, a dozen or so years of life—just a third to a quarter of the engineering life of most public works. Only three of every four projects obligated by mid-1972 were completed two years later. Nevertheless, the Economic Development Administration attempted a longitudinal analysis in 1974 by reconsidering fifty projects that had been evaluated in 1970. All were at least six years old.[27] A separate study of industrial parks reviewed the changes in their utilization between 1971 and 1974.[28]

The reevaluation covered thirty-two water and sewer, ten industrial and commercial and eight miscellaneous projects. Overall, the number of jobs directly associated with the projects grew by 35 percent in the four-year period.[29] The bulk of the growth was associated with industrial and commercial projects in which employment grew by over 150 percent in contrast with a 16 percent increase in the jobs connected with water and sewer projects. Yet in both cases the 1974 job totals exceeded the estimates predicted in 1970. Water and sewer projects showed lower results because about a third of those included served mainly residential customers and many of the industrial and commercial users were established businesses less apt to grow. Industrial and commercial projects, on the other hand, included eight industrial park projects. Employment growth can be traced to greater utilization in at least half the cases. The survey of fifty-three industrial parks supports the notion that over time Economic Development Administration supported industrial parks have had at least limited success in attracting new tenants. Between 1971 and 1974, the average utilization rate rose from 35 to 53 percent of developed acreage.[30]

Because most Economic Development Administration projects involve a one-time investment of federal funds, it is clear that as benefits increase over the life of the investment, benefit-cost calculations become more favorable. In the ten industrial and commercial projects mentioned above, costs per direct job created fell from over $13,000 to just over $5,100. Water and sewer costs to the agency per direct job also fell by 14 percent for the thirty-two cases.

The growth associated with the fifty projects reevaluated in 1974 may reflect the impact of overall growth in the project areas. Population in those areas receiving aid rose by 2.1 percent between 1970 and 1972, up from 1.3 percent for the previous five-year period. Yet unemployment in many of the areas was accelerating. Moreover, it is important to maintain a perspective on the role that the growth associated with the Economic Development Administration's public works plays in relation to overall employment in the community. For example, after a 90-acre Biddeford, Maine, industrial park was completed with the help of a 1968 grant, eight companies providing 417 jobs associated with the project by 1974 moved in. Although the jobs created have all gone to county residents, represented new types of occupations for the county and were in firms manufacturing goods to be exported for sale—all positive factors in long term structural economic change—it is important to remember that the jobs represented less than 1 percent of 1972 total employment in the county.

Another long term benefit occurs when communities are encouraged by participation in an Economic Development Administration project to advance other economic development efforts. In the case of the fifty projects included in the 1974 study the results are mixed, and because of the subjective nature of the information collected, it is almost impossible to conclude whether the Economic Development Administration's involvement had any lasting impact. Considering the agency's limited resources and widespread clientele, only a few communities can match the record of Duluth, Minnesota, or Seattle, Washington, which have compiled long lists of agency-funded projects. Duluth has received five public works grants totaling $6 million, technical assistance projects, and a $772,000 business loan. The development activities include port facilities, a convention center, and trade fair activities. Seattle's $11.6 million in public works grants cover port facilities, an educational facility, a civic center, sewers and street improvements. Minority development organizations have received several technical assistance grants. In either case it is difficult to separate the effects of potent congressional representation affecting economic development legislation or improved grantsmanship from better city planning and execution of economic development activities.

Beyond Just Projects?

"We are not in the water and sewer business; we are in the business of selling ideas" became a favorite slogan of the Assistant Secretary of Commerce for Economic Development who served during the early 1970s. The statement reflected the hope that the Economic Development Administration could do more than fund public works projects whose benefits outweighed costs. The goal was to stimulate community economic development that would complement the agency's projects.

As was discussed in Chapter 4, this desired economic development "process" has been difficult to attain in many areas since project-by-project grantsmanship is easier to achieve than comprehensive and coordinated planning, especially if carrying out the plan involves rejection of a tempting federal grant. Overcoming the project-by-project approach to grant approval and management also has been difficult for agency administrators in Washington and the regional offices.

However, lessons were learned. For example, the self-evaluation of industrial park projects advised against investing in several small parks in the same vicinity when somewhat larger parks were more likely to succeed. Moreover, the report suggested that the utilization of industrial parks probably could be increased if business loans and promotional assistance were available in concert with the bricks and mortar of site development.[31] Although none of these revelations is earthshaking, the findings reflect a failure by both administrators and local representatives to go beyond a project-by-project approach to economic development and look at what else is occurring in the community and what combination of tools are required for success. These criticisms of the industrial park projects led the agency's

Office of Public Works to attempt to implement a policy calling for development of existing parks first and requiring a more careful review of other activities in the same area by local and regional economic development representatives before applying for a public works grant.

Countercyclical Public Works

Three times since the passage of the Area Redevelopment Act in 1961 Congress added a countercyclical public works program to the responsibilities of the federal agency for economic development: the Accelerated Public Works Program (APW) in 1962, the Public Works Impact Program (PWIP) in 1971, and the Job Opportunities Program (Title X of the Public Works and Economic Development Act) in 1974. In each case the program was intended to create immediate jobs for those forced into idleness by a recession or short term setback in the local economy; long term development was secondary. Total outlays in each of these programs amounted to:

	(millions)
Accelerated Public Works (fiscal 1963-1966)	$836.0
Public Works Impact Program (fiscal 1972-1974)	129.9
Job Opportunities Program (fiscal 1975-1976, appropriated)	500.0

The most common projects funded under the first two programs were water and sewer lines, streets, roads, and municipal buildings.[32] Under both laws projects were to be started as quickly as possible and were to be judged on their short run job creation impact during construction, but it is likely that many could have been justified on a long term development basis as broadly defined by the economic development legislation.

The Job Creation Impact

During 1963 the Area Redevelopment Administration and the Community Facilities Administration figured the cost per man-month of on-site employment in Accelerated Public Works projects at almost $700.[33] Projected to cover the entire $850 million appropriated, these rough estimates promised over a million man-months (or more than 93,000 man-years) of on-site work. But a General Accounting Office review a year later revealed the actual job creation impact fell more than halfway short of the goal.[34] Although it has since been discontinued, technological advancement in data processing allowed for closer tabs to be kept on the first 653 PWIP projects. A sample of 202 PWIP undertakings in fiscal 1972 and 1973 averaged more than $3,700 per man-month on-site employment.[35] Moreover, less than a third of the man-months of work created went to target group employees, and many of the opportunities were filled by those from outside the impacted area. The Economic Development Administration did only slightly better than its predecessor in forecasting the jobs created by the program. EDA predicted over 62,000 man-months of on-site employment for the first two years of the program; only 39,000 man-months were realized.

When potential jobs created or income earned from the orders placed for bricks and mortar to build these public works projects is considered, on-site employment underestimates the full impact of the program. Multiplier effects, which are difficult to estimate, must also be taken into account. When the total job creation of public works is considered, the differentials with other programs may not be as great as is frequently asserted by analysts who have estimated costs only on the basis of jobs created on site. Moreover, public works allows the utilization of a greater variety of skills, can stimulate the construction industry that often suffers greatly in recession, and can leave a legacy of useful streets, water lines, and public buildings for future generations.

The Immediacy of Job Creation

The countercyclical public works programs suffered from time lags along the way from the proposal to legislative action and then to the expenditure of funds. President Kennedy requested funds in February 1962, and the Accelerated Public Works program passed in September as unemployment, then 5.7 percent, was on the decline from its 8.1 percent peak in February. The first $400 million were appropriated that fall, and another $450 million the following spring. The Area Redevelopment Administration expected the bulk of the projects to start within five months of approval. As it turned out, when all the lags combined, over three-fourths of the APW expenditures occurred in fiscal years 1964 and 1965.[36] Although unable to forecast the recession and take action while economic conditions were declining, Congress and the administration were able to provide assistance during the recovery.

When PWIP was approved in August 1971, the seasonally adjusted unemployment rate was 6.1 percent, almost the same level as in December when over half of the first fiscal year's projects were approved. Most projects got underway in less than 3 1/2 months during the first fiscal year. The second year's funds became available in the fall of 1972 when Congress refunded the program. Therefore, both waves of PWIP expenditures resulted in employment peaks during the summers of 1972 and 1973 respectively, coinciding with seasonal construction peaks. Again, unemployment had peaked around the time the legislation was enacted and was falling as the initial program gathered steam.

Can It Work?

Countercyclical public works programs were too small and too late to play an important role in the brief recessions of 1961 and 1971. These experiences suggest that to maximize the effectiveness of countercyclical public works Congress would do well to consider a trigger mechanism that would release funds in the early stages of a recession rather than to postpone expenditures until recovery is underway. In a longer and deeper slump as in 1974 and 1975 the problem of time lags may not prove crucial, and Congress may have acted profitably after the onslaught of the recession.

Countercyclical public works have become popular in Congress. In 1974 Congress fought off an administration request to end PWIP, but did cut the proportion of public works funds to be spent on it from a minimum of 25 to 10 percent. Then faced with a severely slumping economy, the Job Opportunities Program was added to the law in December. The first $125 million of the $500 authorized was appropriated and obligated by June 1975; the other $375 million followed in fiscal 1976. With that provision scheduled to expire, Congress has proposed an even larger commitment of $2.5 billion through September 1977—a proposal sure to receive close scrutiny from the deficit-sensitive Ford administration.

7

Business Development

Overshadowed by the public works program are the complementary forms of economic assistance included under the Public Works and Economic Development Act. Business loans and guarantees date from Senator Douglas' original depressed-area proposal under which aid to private business was to play a leading role. Other programs to help areas adjust to economic decline caused by trade agreements, military closings, rail abandonment, and other economic reversals have gained recognition, although few funds, in the more recent legislation.

None of these measures has ever been funded on an equal basis with public works. Cumulative business loan obligations, exclusive of $141 million in guarantees through September 1975, amounted to $413 million. The program peaked at $52 million in fiscal 1968 and again in 1973; appropriations in 1976 totalled $58 million, including $17 million funded under the 1974 Trade Act. Title IX, which provides for grants for economic adjustment planning and implementation was funded at $38.8 million in 1975, and $77 million in 1976 including $15 million set aside for trade adjustment assistance.

Business Development Program

The Economic Development Act's business development program is a federal credit program to help private business and, in a few cases, public bodies and Indian tribes in designated areas with direct loans to build, expand or renovate industrial or commercial facilities, guarantees for working capital loans financed by private lending institutions, and collateral protection expenditures. The 1974 amendments expanded the program, enabling the Economic Development Administration to guarantee fixed asset loans and leases as well as to make loans for working capital. This latter expansion of the means available for business development was intended to help save jobs in companies that could not survive without adequate working capital as well as financing for expansion.

125

Legislative Standards for Loans

The debate preceding passage of the Area Redevelopment Act of 1961 established the basic criteria for the business loan program, and with some exceptions the Economic Development Act's program has much the same rationale and standards. Initially the Economic Development Administration was to act as a lender of last resort by making funds available to business enterprises unable to arrange conventional financing. The terms, determined by the agency, will allow the project to be completed either because of a shortage of funds in the area or because the risk is too high. In addition, if the Small Business Administration, Farmers Home Administration, or any other federal source will make the loan, the applicant must try there first. Nonetheless, Congress did not want the agency to take excessive risks, and it can make loans only on projects that provide a reasonable assurance of repayment. The agency is forbidden from lending to firms in industries where sufficient capacity exists. Moreover, firms applying must demonstrate that the undertaking will contribute to the permanent alleviation of unemployment in a designated depressed area. Aid to corporations with branch plants raised the spectre of runaway shops; government assistance might contribute to unemployment in one area in order to create jobs elsewhere. For that reason, the agency limits loans to new branches of existing firms as long as no unemployment would result in the company's other branches.

If the drafters of the Economic Development Act had limited the agency to last resort lending, they also would have tied the agency's hands and prevented it from carrying out its function of rehabilitating depressed areas. The law, therefore, allows some flexibility in the decision to make loans to businesses if conventional terms are not adequate to complete the project. Loans can be approved for larger corporations with more solid financial backing to induce them to locate in designated areas.[1]

Advocates of the Economic Development Administration's loan policies insist that the restrictions imposed upon the agency are manageable and business development aid could play a more important role in economic development. But program administrators and Congress preferred less controversial public works to loans that could give a competitive advantage to private businesses and thus raise objections from established firms. When Congress rejected the Nixon administration proposal to terminate the Economic Development Act, the Office of Management and Budget considered the loan program the most vulnerable and cut it drastically. More recently business loans recovered the lost ground, but by the end of 1975 it was not clear whether the loan program will recapture the prominent position it held initially in the arsenal of tools to help labor surplus areas.

Loans can be made for up to twenty-five years, although as of 1975 the average maturity was less than twenty years. The duration is determined on a case-by-case basis considering the useful life of the physical plant, the marketable life of the product, the expected profit stream, and the nature of the project. The interest rate is based on the average market yield on U.S. Treasury obligations of similar maturity and is adjusted quarterly. Over its first decade the Economic Development Administration's loan rate averaged well below the market prime, but more recently it has exceeded the rate charged by private banks to prime borrowers.

There is a 65 percent ceiling on the Economic Development Administration's participation, excluding other federal aid to the project. At least 15 percent must be put up by the firm in the form of equity capital or a loan inferior to the agency's. One-third of that amount must come in the form of state or community development corporation participation, or, if that is not available, from the applicant or another nonfederal source. In most cases the agency has limited its share of project costs to one-half, and even less when a larger corporation is involved.

Economic Development Act funds have accounted for just over 46 percent of the total amount on business loan projects funded between fiscal 1966 and 1975.[2] Banks put up another 20 percent and applicants and other private sources 14 percent each. The balance was supported by other sources including local development, state and county fund-raising efforts.

As of September 30, 1975 the Economic Development Administration's portfolio consisted of 427 business loans—261 made by that agency plus 166 of Area Redevelopment Administration vintage. Repayments are made to a so-called "revolving" fund account with the U.S. Treasury. The term is misleading, however, since the agency has never received authorization from the Office of Management and Budget to dip into the fund for new projects. In the fall of 1975 the fund consisted of $106.8 million collected on Area Redevelopment

Act loans and $34.5 million from Economic Development Act loans (Table 7-1).

When a recipient is unable to make loan payments several options are open. The Economic Development Administration can defer payments on the principal and can extend a working capital guarantee in hopes of nursing the business back to health. The agency also can subordinate its lien position or release some of its collateral to the borrower for security on new capital from another nonfederal source. Other possibilities include arrangements for mergers or infusion of additional equity capital. In 1975, the 17 Area Redevelopment Act loans on which payments were deferred totalled $2.3 million in principal payments due while the 49 Economic Development Act loans had an outstanding balance of $43.0 million in principal.

Liquidation, which results in a loss to the federal government, has occurred in 149 cases and was in progress in 25 others (Figure 7-1). Whether the Economic Development Administration's loans will eventually fall into the Area Redevelopment Administration's pattern of over one-fourth of the loans ending in liquidation is subject

Table 7-1

The Economic Development Administration's Loan Portfolio, September 30, 1975 (millions)

Loan Status	Total	ARA	EDA
Total	$495.3	$169.4	$325.8
Revolving fund account	141.2	106.8	34.5
Undisbursed obligations	34.0	–	34.0
Principal receivable:			
Payments current	216.2	43.3	172.9
Payments deferred	45.3	2.3	43.0
Past due	30.2	12.1	18.1
In liquidation	18.3	3.5	14.8
Other assets:			
Defaulted working capital loans purchased	3.0	–	3.0
Accrued interest	6.5	1.3	5.2
Collateral property acquired	0.5	0.1	0.3

Note: Details do not add to totals due to rounding.
Source: U.S. Department of Commerce, Economic Development Administration, Office of Business Development, *Management Information Report as of September 30, 1975*, November 12, 1975 (mimeo.), p. 1.

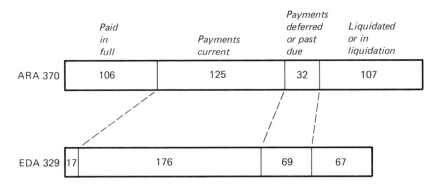

Source: U.S. Department of Commerce, Economic Development Administration, Office of Business Development, *Management Information Report as of September 30, 1975* November 12, 1975 (mimeo.), pp. 1, 6.

Figure 7-1. Status of Area Redevelopment Act and Economic Development Act Business Loans, Cumulative to September 30, 1975.

to speculation. Firms with Area Redevelopment Administration loans have had longer opportunity to be hit by economic hardship, and even in 1975 liquidation proceedings on four of these loans were less than a year old. Only time will tell if the Economic Development Administration can improve on the Area Redevelopment Administration's record.

The losses from the liquidation of business loans amounted to $33.7 million in principal and $3.1 million in interest on the ninety-eight Area Redevelopment Act loans and $16.9 million in principal and $0.8 million in interest on the fifty-one Economic Development Act loans. This gross loss of $54.5 million should be reduced by proceeds from the sale of acquired collateral but the recovery has been slight—$0.4 million. Judgments in connection with liquidation cost the government another $2.9 million for Area Redevelopment Act loans and $0.4 million for Economic Development Act loans. The net result has been a loss of $39.3 million by the Area Redevelopment Administration—or a quarter of the program's disbursements—and $18.4 million by the Economic Development Administration—5 percent of obligations.

Although these loan losses are large when judged by normal banking standards, it is not clear where a federal agency should draw the line on accepting losses on socially desirable, but high risk investments. The Economic Development Administration believes in bending backwards to put off foreclosure as long as possible in hopes of avoiding closing a business. A less sympathetic policy would have saved money, but would not be in the spirit of the law.

Other Business Development Tools

The agency also guarantees working capital loans for the businesses to whom loans had been made. Through September 1975 it had guaranteed 102 loans for a total $141 million, and in several instances the same firm received more than one. Nearly half of that amount was secured in fiscal 1975 when the agency guaranteed twelve loans amounting to $68 million. Guarantees cannot cover more than 90 percent of the unpaid balance of the business loan.

Funds are obligated into a reserve fund in case the agency must pick up the tab for a defaulted guarantee. Until 1972, 25 percent of the agency's guarantee had to be covered by the fund. It was lowered to 10 percent in 1972 and raised again to 20 percent in 1975. If the current fiscal year obligations are insufficient to cover defaults, previous years' reserves are available. Thirty-nine of the eighty-one working capital loans guaranteed between fiscal 1966 and 1973 had defaulted by September 1975 at a cost to the agency of $14.8 million. Allowing for seven loans on which $3.0 million in outstanding principal may yet be paid and $0.3 million recovered on the others, the losses made up by the taxpayer totalled $11.5 million, or two-thirds as much as under the business loan program. Working capital losses accounted for 17 percent of authorized guarantees and 66 percent of the reserved funds.

The 1974 amendments broadened the scope of the business development program to allow both guarantees and loans for land, facilities, equipment and working capital, as well as guarantees of up to 90 percent of rental payments remaining on leases. The lease guarantee provision is aimed largely at encouraging the use of vacant urban buildings and supplements a similar program under the Small Business Administration. No lease guarantees were approved as of late 1975 because, according to agency officials, many of the applications appeared to be attempts at real estate speculation, not job creation.

Even though Congress was aware of the record of the working capital guarantees, it opened the door to more guaranteed loans because they are a cheaper form of business aid. Considering the limited business development budget, an expanded use of these guarantees stretches the budget dollar. Moreover, in a recession, the aim was to provide the agency the flexibility to help firms on the verge of going out of business—that is to say, to save jobs—as well as aiding expansion and new businesses. Two examples are a guarantee of a $22.5 million working capital loan by a thirteen-bank consortium to .Todd Shipyards Corporation of New York City and the guarantees of $6.5 million on private loans to Eagle International, Inc., a bus manufacturer in Brownsville, Texas. In the Todd case, the funds were applied to the operations of shipyards in the San Pedro area of Los Angeles and in Seattle, which employ 4,200 persons. The impact of inflation on the cost of building eight tankers under a fixed cost contract plus the 1974 oil embargo had caused such a serious drain on Todd's cash flow that closings and employment losses of up to 10,000 were threatened. Eagle's financial distress was the result of a ruling by the state of Texas that the city could not sell industrial revenue bonds to establish the operations in two aircraft hangars belonging to the city. In both cases the jobs saved are located in the Economic Development Administration's designated areas, and private financing would have been denied without the agency's guarantee.

Administering Business Loans

As of 1975, decision making in the business development program was centralized to a great degree in Washington although regional office representatives assisted potential lenders in developing applications. The agency plans, however, to allow regional offices to begin to process loans directly. Negotiations with banks and coordination with other federal loan programs normally are handled regionally. As in the public works program regional office negotiations can weed out applicants unlikely to be approved. Loan applications sent on to Washington not only are scrutinized for credit soundness, but also must pass several other tests. EDA must satisfy the Environmental Protection Agency that the new business will not violate environmental standards, and the applicant's affirmative action plan must be approved. A third requirement is evidence assuring that sufficient demand exists for the goods or services to be produced and that existing capacity could not absorb the increased output.

The time required to reach a final decision on a business loan has been blamed for discouraging potentially qualified applicants from approaching the agency for funds. Between fiscal 1966 and 1971 the median processing time ranged from 296 to 186 days.[3] More recently the delay has been cut to three months or less. Agency officials assign responsibility for delays to a shortage of staff and the length of time it takes to do the additional studies after the application is filed. Fulfilling the requirement that two conventional lenders must turn down the project also can add to the wait.

The requirement for a study of capacity and demand rarely has been used in the public works program, where there is often no advance notice about the firms that would locate in connection with the project. However, such a study is always done for a business loan. In several instances—for example, a television tube manufacturer and a cotton mill—they were negative. But positive findings are no insurance against future problems, and the agency has been sued a number of times by angry competitors claiming existing industry capacity is both adequate and efficient.

Besides requirements to meet civil rights, environmental standards, and a capacity study, business development recipients face restrictions on the salaries they pay their officers, fixed assets expenditures, and dividends paid. Financial statements must be submitted quarterly to the agency. These and other duties and obligations of loan recipients vary little from conventional loan practices.

Firms also must provide assurances that they are not runaways— having closed in one location within the last two years to reopen with the Economic Development Administration's aid elsewhere. Branches of larger corporations seeking loan assistance must show that they have not shut down or reduced employment in a similar facility. Once located with the agency's help, a company withdrawing from the designated area faces a recall of its loan. A more likely scenario is for a failing company to go under and then reopen with better management and capitalization. In only a few cases that one eleven-year veteran of the loan program could remember did bankruptcy and the loss of the loan also mean the permanent closing of the facility.

Because the Economic Development Administration's loan program parallels that of the Small Business Administration (SBA), a working agreement between the two agencies calls for applicants for loans under $350,000 to be referred to SBA first. The arrangement reflects the different purposes of the two agencies. SBA is in the business of encouraging small entrepreneurs. The Economic Development Administration, on the other hand, is mandated to take into account the jobs created before potential profits accruing to management.

The desire to raise the job impact of Economic Development Act loans and the need to adjust for inflation were the major reasons for the increased size of the average business loan from under $700,000 in fiscal 1966 to $1.4 million in fiscal 1971 and $1.5 million in fiscal 1974. Another important consideration was the belief that larger loans to well-established corporations would be less risky since management skills and financial support would be available from the parent corporation.

Inadequate management has been singled out as the leading cause of business failure and loan losses. In terms of the total costs of the loan program—administration, loan losses and the opportunity costs of investing taxpayer's dollars at lower rates than the private market will pay—a recent review of the first five years of the program under the Economic Development Administration estimated losses to account for 9 percent of the costs. About one-fifth of the loans in that period, or one-seventh of the funds were liquidated. Half of those, especially the large ones, since they accounted for 80 percent of the funds, reopened.

Some apparently economically sound plans still did not guarantee success. One of the most disappointing losses was a sugar beet processing plant in Easton, Maine, which received a $2.3 million business loan and a $1.8 million working capital guarantee in 1966. The novel and seemingly logical idea behind the enterprise was to diversify the crop of area potato farmers to include sugar beets. When the strong-willed farmers continued producing the one crop they knew best, the company attempted to import sugar beets from other parts of the country and even explored the possibility of shifting to cane, but transportation proved too expensive. After another working capital guarantee, and several feasibility studies, the company closed. An idea that looked feasible on paper and made economic sense in theory just did not suit the farmers of Maine in practice.

An Assessment

Evaluations of the Economic Development Administration's business loan program have been limited, and while the studies have addressed a variety of issues, some important considerations have been barely touched. One of the first problems in quantifying the costs and benefits of loans is to define costs to allow for the fact that money is repaid with interest. The true cost of the business loan program to EDA, and consequently to the taxpayer, is not the loan amount but the opportunity costs of lending funds at lower rates when higher market yields could be achieved, the losses on business failures not repaid, and the administrative costs of servicing the loans for up to twenty-five years. Benefits can be measured in much the same manner as for public works projects—the number of jobs created and the wages paid to new employees.

The usefulness of benefit-cost studies is impaired by the myriad of variables involved in selecting the proper social discount rate with which to calculate the present value of opportunity costs, determining the lifespan of cost and benefit streams, and measuring indirect income gains due to multiplier effects. Studies of the Economic Development Administration's loan program are a good illustration of the confusing answers policy makers can receive when they raise questions about cost-effectiveness. A 1968 study of eight loans made during both the Area Redevelopment Act era and under the first two years of the Economic Development Act found benefits exceeded costs from 12:1 to 25:1.[4] An effort to repeat the analysis for a sample of 40 loans of $100,000 or more made before fiscal 1969 computed benefit-cost figures anywhere from a situation where benefits are slightly less than costs to 20:1.[5] The higher estimates reflect counting the income from every new job in the firm (not just income increases or jobs for the poor and unemployed) regardless of the Economic Development Administration's portion of total investment, lower social discount rates, and higher multiplier estimates. Still another variation on the benefit-cost theme, which reviewed 44 firms involved in the agency's program as of fiscal 1970, yielded an almost unbelievable ratio of 53:1.[6] Preliminary results of a 1975 study estimated that for every dollar it cost the agency for 186 loans made between 1966 and 1970, the firms will generate over the eighteen-year average lifespan of the loans almost $30 in wages, tax payments, sales, and purchases of supplies. Without passing judgment on the precision of these estimates, the only practical conclusion from these studies is that prudent business loans will likely pay for themselves in added income and economic growth.

The fact that loans create jobs and income tell only part of the story. If the program is to achieve its mission, it is necessary to determine if the loan program locates job opportunities where the needy will benefit and if it avoids supplanting available private sector financing. A closer look should, therefore, be taken at the types of jobs created, the distribution of the benefits and the financial situations of the firms assisted.

As was true in many public works projects, the majority of workers taking jobs in firms helped by the business loan program had been employed previously. Most were residents of the county where the firm was located. The quality of jobs created has varied. The 1969 survey found half of the new employees still among the working poor.[7] Those surveyed in 1970 averaged close to $6,000 per job, still slightly lower than the annual national average in manufacturing.[8] During the early years of the program, loans were typically for pulp, paper, and plywood industries, food processing plants and furniture manufacturers, but over the years they have run the gamut from ski resorts to a turkey processing plant.

Since so many of the new employees of the firms assisted under the loan program had been employed previously, a survey of the jobs they left was taken to see if employment there filtered down to the unemployed. In a sample of 1,742 jobs in thirty-one firms financed by the business loan program, seven of every ten jobs were filled by previously employed workers.[9] Of the jobs they left, a third were filled by the previously employed, a fifth by the unemployed, and the remainder were jobs that disappeared. Therefore, the net job creation impact of the loans to the thirty-one firms when the secondary impact is considered was 80 percent of the number of new jobs in agency-assisted firms. Without more detailed studies of the jobs that disappeared, it is impossible to tell whether the "musical chairs" job shifts were assisting workers in declining industries whose jobs eventually would have been lost.

Business Loan Issues

Direct federal aid to private business enterprises is seen by skeptics as an unnecessary interference with the private market, a view that is commonly nourished by conventional lenders. Economic Development Administration officials choose to see their program not as a way of supplanting the market mechanism but as a way of leveraging private funds to be involved in more business undertakings.

The shortage of venture capital is a major impediment to the rehabilitation of rural depressed areas. Sources of funds from outside the area shun the high risk. Locally, incomes are too low to be saved and, in turn, loaned. And, what money is made in these areas often is invested in more prosperous localities. The Economic Development Administration's role is small in rural areas in comparison to that of other federal lenders. SBA loans in nonmetropolitan areas in fiscal 1973 stood at over $600 million—more than six times the Economic Development Administration's obligated funds in nonmetropolitan areas.[10] Under a new program authorizing the Department of Agriculture's Farmer's Home Administration to guarantee industrial and business loans in areas of 50,000 or fewer persons, $200 million was guaranteed in fiscal 1974.[11]

The Economic Development Administration's role is changing, then, to one of providing loans to larger businesses with experienced management and better collateral. These are cases where even the banks have refused to take a chance on the full loan, but are induced to provide credit if the Economic Development Administration's participation or guarantee is secured. In urban areas where the argument that credit facilities are in short supply does not apply, the agency is lending and guaranteeing funds for risky or minority-run projects.

There is a fine line between acting as a lender of last resort and making high risk loans to viable business. The agency may help those turned down by the private market, but must weigh applicants' ability to repay the loan in much the same manner as a banker. Each loan application is negotiated separately, but on a first come, first served basis. Nothing ensures that the Economic Development Administration will select the next thirty or fifty best ventures that the private market could not serve. In each case the agency must weigh the demand to use tax dollars most effectively against the mandate to absorb the risk conventional lenders refuse to bear.

Business development loans and guarantees, by their nature, are long-run development projects. Jobs are expected to last at least the life of the loan, although there have been a few cases where businesses have paid off their debt to the Economic Development Administration and left the area.

The program has shifted emphasis with the addition of the broader selection of vehicles in fiscal 1975 to include countercyclical activities—saving existing jobs in companies suffering from the recession.

A bird-in-hand seems to be more appealing than a promise of things to come. Congress took little interest in business loans for job creation and reduced the program to $17 million in fiscal 1975 but raised the amount to $58 million for fiscal 1976 (including trade adjustment) when the agency promised to save existing jobs. Business development officials claim their fan mail from the Hill has picked up with the new loans and guarantees made to save jobs, but it is highly unlikely that loans will ever replace public works as the favorite among economic development programs.

The job saving aspect of the loan program, particularly guarantees that can more easily be expanded and contracted, should not be allowed to supplant the long run nature of the program as the economy approaches full capacity again. The danger is that economic development funds would be used to shore up sagging businesses rather than to promote new enterprises in good times. Adjustment to permanent, not countercyclical, economic decline should take the form of reusing facilities or protecting workers from plant closings and retraining them for new opportunities. How the agency will choose to modify its economic adjustment policy in a post-recession economy is an important question for the future.

In considering the business loan program it is significant to note that the federal government has few other means to help industries locating in depressed areas. Wage or location subsidies, which are utilized in many European countries, have not been tested in this country despite the evidence that firms respond to wage differences in choosing locations. Differential tax treatment is left to state and local development legislation except in times of war. Although from an economic standpoint experiments along these lines might provide useful policy tools, they are politically inferior to loans and guarantees that will not tend to give long run competitive advantages to any individual firm since they must be repaid.

It is possible that when federal, state, and local efforts are considered, the federal role in influencing private business location directly is small. State industrial development authorities are active across the nation. Tax policies, such as breaks on the taxes paid on the salaries of nonmanagement employees in Vermont to attract employers or a lower inventory tax in North Carolina to ward off the loss of textile plants, are debated each year in state legislatures.[12] In contrast, the importance of the Economic Development Administration's program of, perhaps, fewer than fifty loans annually, is diminished.

Economic Adjustment Program

Title IX, the economic adjustment program, enacted in 1974 is a modified version of the Nixon administration proposal for replacing the Economic Development Act with a block grant program to states to plan and conduct economic adjustment projects. The administration argued that the Economic Development Administration had done little to revive declining areas and might be more effective in preventing decline. Congress disagreed with the first half of the administration argument, but agreed that an economic adjustment program was worth trying. Under Title IX the agency can make grants to states and localities for projects to help an area overcome a structural economic dislocation caused by the action of the federal government, an environmental ruling or any other severe conditions—such as a national disaster, foreign competition, or permanent plant closings due to shifts in technology.

Title IX drops the pretext of bolstering depressed areas and, although administered by the Economic Development Administration, this aid is not limited to designated areas. Economic adjustment funds may be used to support projects that the other forms of assistance cannot accommodate. Where an adverse change in economic conditions threatens an existing federal project, the agency might apply economic adjustment dollars to the problem. An example occurred when a $3 million grant was extended to a consortium of fifteen Indian tribes in the Dakotas and Montana—the site of a sizeable federal investment in Indian cattleraising. The Title IX funds were intended to help the tribes replace losses sustained during a severe storm.

The sixteen demonstration areas funded under the economic adjustment program with the $35.4 million allotted in fiscal 1975 and those for which planning got underway in fiscal 1976 have called for more traditional types of economic development assistance. In Wood County, West Virginia, for example, where a major plant closed owing to a technological change in tire production that eliminated the need for rayon, 1775 jobs were lost. An industrial park, improvements in the water system, and development of a recreation site are planned to compensate.

A less orthodox use of a Title IX grant is the case of South Bend, Indiana. There, the city turned the money into a $5 million loan to an employee stock-ownership trust, which took over South Bend

Lathe rather than let it close, taking 500 jobs with it. The State of Colorado, which qualified for help because its small communities could not keep up with the rapid growth in the state, used its grant dollars to create a loan fund. The state makes water and sewer loans, for example, to communities whose present tax base is insufficient. In both cases, as the loans are repaid with interest, funds can be reloaned for economic adjustment assistance in the future.

Since economic adjustment projects are barely off the ground, it is difficult to tell how effective they will be in warding off economic decline. Although many of the individual projects look much the same as regular public works, technical assistance, and loan program undertakings, Title IX areas can receive larger doses of federal funds. It provides the Economic Development Administration with an opportunity to combine several types of aid under a single grant umbrella. Another possible advantage is that aid can work to salvage an existing economic base when facilities have not fallen into disrepair and workers are still present. However, where the conversion of buildings and skills demands large investments in both new plant and equipment and retraining, the process of development will more closely parallel the experience of the long-term economic development programs that have struggled to have a noticeable impact on the communities assisted. And where the problem is as large as the impact of rail abandonment, the Economic Development Administration is admittedly powerless to act. One project might call for using the entire year's allocation. Possibly to thwart preventive efforts, the Ford administration recommended reducing economic adjustment appropriations to $45 million in fiscal year 1977, a cut of $32 million from the previous year.

8   The Uncertain Balance Sheet

A decade and a half of federal aid to depressed areas has indicated the potential of such efforts as well as the constraints. The passage of the Area Redevelopment Act in 1961 suggested that as a matter of public policy the federal government rejected the Darwinist notion that some ghost towns were inevitable and accepted the idea that the social capital invested in lagging or declining communities could be salvaged. But even before the legislation was enacted and the first dollar spent to aid depressed areas, Congress could not overcome the temptation of trying to feed the multitudes with a few loaves. No miracles were forthcoming, and the limited resources that eight successive Congresses and four administrations allocated were far from adequate to aid the number of counties—half of all counties in the United States—that became eligible for assistance under the program to aid lagging areas.

Because resources were limited, the administrators of aid to depressed areas continually were faced with choosing priorities and selecting the most worthy among equals. Following the social conscience that prompted legislation to aid unemployed persons stranded in chronic labor surplus areas, the obvious inclination was to attend to the needs of the areas worst off. But there was also an understandable drive to achieve visible successes in depressed areas. Otherwise vast investments involving considerable risks would have been necessary before discernible benefits could be achieved.

Congress did what comes naturally and chose to follow a course that would yield the best of all possible worlds. Following its comprehensive review of the initial four-years aid to depressed areas, Congress overhauled the area redevelopment strategy when it passed, in 1965, the Appalachian Regional Development Act and the Public Works and Economic Development Act. Not giving up on aiding chronic labor surplus areas, the economic development legislation also embraced a concept of growth centers that embodied a special application of a trickle-down approach. Instead of helping the depressed areas directly, Congress thought that funds allocated to help lagging areas could be invested in adjoining growth centers, hoping that the spillover would soak up some of the unemployed persons in nearby depressed areas. The assumption was that the newly employed workers would not move out from their communities and that they would continue to utilize the social capital invested in their area of residence.

Whatever the merits and attractions of a growth center strategy, the expectations of advocates did not stand up under the scrutiny of actual experience. A 1972 survey showed that the primary beneficiaries of the jobs funded by the agency in growth centers were the residents in those areas, and that less than 10 percent of the jobs created by Economic Development Act funds in growth centers employed residents of adjoining depressed areas. In addition, the survey showed that hoped-for spillover benefits did not materialize. Suppliers to assisted businesses did not significantly expand employment, and wages earned were spent mainly outside the needy areas.[1] Nevertheless, the Economic Development Administration has continued to encourage the formation of economic development districts.

Aside from the selection of areas, the planners and administrators of aid to labor surplus areas had to face decisions on what types of projects they would approve. Efforts that were directly associated with bringing jobs to depressed areas were of course to be preferred. The question to be decided was what type of projects would spur growth more broadly and more rapidly. Some planners thought that amenity-oriented projects would be most helpful in achieving the desired growth. This meant spending area redevelopment funds for bolstering educational facilities or cultural projects, and to some extent this was done. Agency administrators balked, however, at this approach since they felt that Congress might abandon the support of an agency that fights labor surplus with "culture" or recreation. The administrators felt that politically it would be hard to sell to Congress the notion that the unemployed would be helped by another concert hall or golf course.

In the Appalachian legislation Congress expanded the horizons of aid to lagging areas by providing assistance to whole regions. The underlying rationale for the new approach was that few counties have a sufficiently broad base for economic development and that effective economic planning and development requires the united pulling together of a viable economic area sharing common interest and resources. The Appalachian region was the beneficiary of this approach. But as in the case of assistance to local areas, Congress could not withstand the pressure of various claimants to share in the federal largesse. Consequently, a program, which was initially conceived to aid the depressed and underdeveloped coal regions in central Appalachia, was extended to cover thirteen states reaching as far north as New York and encompassing a population that in 1975 counted 19 million persons as residents of the "depressed" region.

The bulk of the nearly $5 billion that Congress appropriated for the Economic Development Administration and the Appalachian Regional Commission during their first ten years of existence was therefore allocated to bolster the infrastructure in designated communities. Economic Development Act public works funds were mostly allocated to the construction of sewage and water facilities that were associated with bringing in new jobs to the areas. The Appalachian Regional Commission has followed the same route of enhancing the region's infrastructure except that the mainstay of aid to Appalachia was the building of highways and access roads. In the case of Appalachian Regional Commission, however, Congress sweetened the road-building program with contributions to the development of human resources ranging from child care to the vocational training of youths to health care provision for the aged.

Given their meager resources, neither agency could offer much direct aid to chronic labor surplus areas. One substitute for dollars was the promise that planning could rally a wider range of resources. The idea was that city hall and county courthouse officials are presiding over increasingly vast resources. Effective local planning would husband these resources more efficiently and channel them to enhance the economic potential of their communities. The challenge was to plug local planners into the resource allocation decision making process. To strengthen the hands of local economic planners, the federal establishment tried to channel funds other than economic development grants through the local advisory agencies that were presumably in charge of economic planning in their localities. But the best that the "feds" could do was to advise local economic groups about pending grants that might potentially be approved. The federal officials did not have the clout to give the local economic advisory planning committees the power to control the expenditure of these grants.

Closely related to economic planning was technical assistance aimed at allowing localities to explore their economic potential. The technical assistance grants were to act as catalysts in identifying problems and spurring economic development. However, feasibility studies and the like proved to be weak uses for technical assistance funds. More innovative efforts—like operating funds for educational facilities, manpower training projects, and support for minority business institutions—had a higher payoff. But considering their budgetary constraints, the economic development agencies could not go beyond the support of pilot projects.

The Appalachian program added a further incentive to strengthen the role of state and local planners—the supplemental grant. By providing a little extra to the federal share, Appalachian communities were encouraged to seek more sources of federal aid. It is likely that many public facilities now in Appalachia would never have existed in the absence of the supplemental grant program.

The final segment of aid to depressed areas consisted of business loans. A casual review of the first fifteen years of federal business development support would indicate that the basic program has changed little, but a closer examination shows how the program has been adapted to the difficult task of implementing aid to the private sector. In the 1950s, when Senator Douglas was advocating federal aid, he thought that lack of venture capital was at the root of the trouble in poor and depressed areas. Therefore he made loans to new and expanding businesses a cornerstone of his design to aid depressed areas. The provision has remained in the law without much change.

In practice, however, administrative emphasis sanctioned by congressional appropriations have resulted in a radical overhaul in attitudes toward aiding businesses in lagging areas. Conventional lenders opposed governmental competition, owners of established businesses resented the establishment of government sponsored competitors, and congressional bans on moving jobs and investment in excess-capacity industries complicated the program. The selection of worthy applicants was also a very difficult task. Most businessmen would welcome the favorable loan terms made by the Economic Development Administration, but clearly those who might be considered the safest borrowers were not eligible because they presumably could obtain credit elsewhere. The most eligible applicants presented the highest risks and excessive failures would have placed the program in jeopardy. To act as a lender of last resort, the Area Redevelopment Administration and its successor found that many borrowers proved to be poor risks and have defaulted on the loans, further discouraging the business loan program. Another blow was dealt the program when the Nixon administration, realizing that Congress would not abandon the Economic Development Act, succeeded in reducing the business loan budget. The Economic Development Administration has tried to reconcile the mandate to keep high risk firms with the pressure to produce a reasonable balance sheet.

The obvious question that arises is whether the $5 billion expenditures to aid Appalachia and other depressed areas have paid off. It would appear that some objective criteria could be designed to measure the impact of such a large amount of funds. But since the funds were spread thinly in half the counties in the United States over a whole decade, satisfactory measures of their impact are not available. This is not to say that the expended funds have not contributed to the economic development of depressed areas, and certainly many jobs, temporary and permanent, have been created in these areas.

To put the extent of federal aid to depressed areas in the proper perspective, it might be useful to bear in mind that the amount spent under the Economic Development Act and the Appalachian Regional Development Act during the decade about equaled the cost of construction of a metropolitan subway in the District of Columbia. A second helpful comparison might be that unemployment insurance benefits during 1975 alone exceeded by more than four times the total federal aid to depressed areas over a decade.

Another perspective on U.S. economic development programs must focus on the long run. Economic decline will not be reversed overnight, and the evidence suggests that individual projects must be given time to grow. Federally sponsored economic development efforts in the United States are still maturing after fifteen years of experience.

Part of the aging process is learning. Economic development planners and administrators have changed the direction of the program over the years. Redirection of Indian and urban projects toward more realistic goals is an important example. Another is the policy to promote better utilization of existing industrial parks and to avoid those less likely to succeed. Finally, economic adjustment assistance opens the door for aid to areas with a broader range of economic problems and promises to apply some preventive measures. As long as failure brings reevaluation, it is difficult to weigh past mistakes as fully as achievements.

It is doubtful whether any yardstick will ever be designed to provide an objective evaluation of the program. As long as depressed areas exist, alleviating economic distress is a proper concern of the federal government as part of its responsibility to promote the general welfare. This would indicate the need to experiment and, where justified, to expand economic development activities rather than abandon the social capital invested in depressed areas, and thus condone the human deprivation of those stranded in lagging areas.

Notes

Notes

Chapter 1
Economic Development Policies
and Legislation

1. Useful discussions of the issues in economic development policy are provided by John N. Cumberland, *Regional Development: Experiences and Prospects in the United States of America* (Paris: Mouton and Co., 1971), pp. 6-20; and by Gordon C. Cameron, *Regional Economic Development: The Federal Role* (Baltimore: The Johns Hopkins University Press, 1970), pp. 11-37.

2. Norman Wengert, "The Politics of Water Resources Development as Exemplified by TVA," in John R. Moore (ed.), *The Economic Impact of TVA* (Knoxville: The University of Tennessee Press, 1967), pp. 63-68.

3. A brief review of the policies of six countries is included in U.S. Congress, House, *National Growth Policy, Part 2*, selected papers submitted to the Subcommittee on Housing of the Committee on Banking and Currency, 92d Cong., 2d Sess. (Washington: Government Printing Office, 1972), pp. 555-629.

4. Sar A. Levitan, *Federal Aid to Depressed Areas: An Evaluation of the Area Redevelopment Administration* (Baltimore: The Johns Hopkins University Press, 1964).

5. *Economic Report of the President*, January 1962 (Washington: Government Printing Office, 1962), pp. 17-21.

6. Congressional Quarterly Service, *Congress and the Nation 1945-1964* (Washington: Congressional Quarterly Service, 1965), pp. 877-878.

7. Donald N. Rothblatt, *Regional Planning: The Appalachian Experience* (Lexington, Mass.: D.C. Heath, 1971), pp. 24-44.

8. James L. Sundquist, *Politics and Policy: The Eisenhower, Kennedy and Johnson Years* (Washington: The Brookings Institution, 1968), pp. 98-105.

9. *Appalachia, A Report by the President's Appalachian Regional Commission 1964* (Washington: Government Printing Office, 1964), pp. 31-56.

10. Sundquist, *Politics and Policy*, pp. 103-105.

11. *Report to the Congress on the Proposal for an Economic*

Adjustment Program by the Department of Commerce and Office of Management and Budget, Washington, D.C., February 1, 1974 (mimeo.).

Chapter 2
People, Places, and Economic Lag

1. The tape of the census was made available by Dr. Sheldon E. Haber of the Department of Economics, The George Washington University, and computer time was provided by the University's Computer Center.

2. Sar A. Levitan and Barbara Hetrick, *Big Brother's Indian Programs—With Reservations* (New York: McGraw-Hill, Inc., 1971), p. 14.

3. Sar A. Levitan and William B. Johnston, *Indian Giving: Federal Programs for Native Americans* (Baltimore: The Johns Hopkins University Press, 1975), p. 17.

4. Boise Cascade Center for Community Development, *Indian Economic Development, An Evaluation of EDA's Selected Indian Reservation Program*, Vol. I, prepared for U.S. Department of Commerce, Economic Development Administration, July 1972, p. 12.

5. *Appalachia, A Report by the President's Appalachian Regional Commission 1964* (Washington: Government Printing Office, 1964). Data in this report do not cover the areas of Mississippi, New York, and South Carolina later added to the Appalachian region.

6. Appalachian Regional Commission, "Local Government Finances in the Appalachian Region (a Summary of Findings from the 1967 Census of Governments)," Appalachian Program Design Summary GF-1 (mimeo.); and "Local Government Finance in the Appalachian Region 1971/72, and Trends (An Early Summary of Findings from the 1972 Census of Governments)," Appalachian Program Design Summary GF-2, September 1974 (mimeo.).

7. Jerome P. Pickard, "Population Trends in the Appalachian Region, 1970-1973, With Projections to 1980," *Current Regional Reports 6* (Washington: Appalachian Regional Commission, December 1974).

Chapter 3
The Chosen Areas

1. Appalachian Regional Commission, *The Appalachian Experiment 1965-1970* (Washington: The Commission, n.d.), pp. 33-34.

2. U.S. Department of Commerce, Economic Development Administration, *Budget Estimates, Fiscal 1976 Congressional Subcommission*, January 1975 (mimeo.).

3. Kenneth L. Deavers and Henry L. Eskew, "Eligibility Criteria for Economic Development Assistance," *The Research Review*, July 1970, p. 3.

4. T. Nicolaus Tideman, "Defining Area Distress in Unemployment," *Public Policy*, Fall 1973, pp. 441-492.

5. Niles M. Hansen, *Intermediate-Size Cities as Growth Centers: Applications for Kentucky, the Piedmont Crescent, the Ozarks and Texas* (New York: Praeger, 1971).

6. U.S. Department of Commerce, Economic Development Administration, Growth Center Evaluation Task Force, *Program Evaluation: The Economic Development of Administration Growth Center Strategy*, February 1972 (mimeo.), pp. 89-91.

7. U.S. General Accounting Office, *More Reliable Data Needed As A Basis for Providing Federal Assistance to Economically Distressed Areas*, No. B-133182, May 10, 1971.

8. James R. Wetzel and Martin Ziegler, "Measuring Unemployment in States and Local Areas," *Monthly Labor Review*, June 1974, pp. 40-46.

Chapter 4
Economic Development Organizations:
Links in the Federal Chain

1. Donald R. Gilmore, *Developing the "Little" Economies*, Supplementary Paper No. 10 (New York: Committee for Economic Development, April 1960), pp. 13-22.

2. U.S. Department of Commerce, Economic Development Administration, *Budget Estimates, Fiscal Year 1977* (Washington: EDA, 1976), pp. EDA-32.

3. U.S. Department of Commerce, Economic Development Administration, Office of Development Organizations, "Economic Development District Survey Report (Sources of Funding and Board Composition, 1974-1975)," pp. 2-3 (mimeo.).

4. Warren T. Zitzmann, *Evaluation of State Development Planning in Appalachia* (draft report) (Washington: Appalachian Regional Commission, January 21, 1971), pp. 41-43 (mimeo.).

5. Robert R. Nathan Associates, Inc., *Evaluation of Economic Development District and Area Planning Programs*, Vol. I, prepared for the U.S. Department of Commerce, Economic Development Administration, January 31, 1969, Chapter IV, p. 8; and U.S. Department of Commerce, Economic Development Administration, Program Evaluation, *Summary of Case Studies: Evaluation of Rural Economic Development Activities in Fifteen Areas*, Spring 1970 (mimeo.), pp. 8-11.

6. Appalachian Regional Commission, *The Local Development District Program* (staff draft), n.d. This report is one of a series of evaluations undertaken between 1969 and 1972.

7. Advisory Commission on Intergovernmental Relations, *Regional Decision Making: New Strategies for Substate Districts* (Washington: Government Printing Office, October 1973), Appendix Table II-A.

8. Martha Derthick, *Between State and Nation: Regional Organizations of the United States* (Washington: The Brookings Institution, 1974), pp. 112-115.

9. New England Regional Commission, *Regional Plan Summary* (Boston: New England Regional Commission, n.d.), p. 17.

10. Robert T. Murphy, "The Regional Commission System," *Public Administration Review*, March/April 1973, p. 184.

11. U.S. Department of Commerce, Economic Development Administration, Program Analysis Division, *A Preliminary Examination of EDA Feasibility Studies*, April 1971 (mimeo.), p. 108.

12. Centaur Management Consultants, Inc., *Evaluation of the Impact of Tourism/Recreation Projects for Economic Development Administration, Vol. I: Results and Methodology*, prepared for U.S. Department of Commerce, Economic Development Administration, June 1973 (mimeo.), p. xxi.

13. U.S. Department of Commerce, Economic Development Administration, *Evaluation of Seven Major Technical Assistance Projects with National Scope*, October 1971 (mimeo.), pp. 4-9.

14. U.S. Department of Labor, Manpower Administration, *Evaluation Study of MDTA Section 241 Program*, Special Evaluation Group Report No. 26, December 1972 (mimeo.).

15. U.S. Congress, House, *Evaluation of Economic Development Programs—Part II*, Hearings before the Special Subcommittee on Economic Development Programs of the Committee on Public Works, 91st Cong., 2d Sess. (Washington: Government Printing Office, 1970), pp. 101-105.

Chapter 5
The Appalachian Program

1. Derthick, *Between State and Nation: Regional Organizations of the United States*,(Washington: The Brookings Institution, 1974), p. 94.

2. Brinley J. Lewis, "New Subregional Budget Approach Gives States More Flexibility," *Appalachia*, August-September 1974, pp. 1-9.

3. Ibid., p. 9.

4. *Appalachia, A Report by the President's Appalachian Regional Commission, 1964* (Washington: Government Printing Office, 1964), p. 32.

5. John Munro, "Planning the Appalachian Development Highway System: Some Critical Questions," *Land Economics*, May 1969, p. 158.

6. Ibid., p. 157.

7. U.S. Bureau of the Census, *Statistical Abstract of the United States, 1973* (Washington: Government Printing Office, 1973), Table 673, p. 423.

8. *1973 Annual Report of the Appalachian Regional Commission* (Washington: The Commission, 1973), p. 23.

9. Carl W. Hale and Joe Walters, "Appalachian Regional Development and the Distribution of Benefits," *Growth and Change*, January 1974, pp. 3-11.

10. U.S. General Accounting Office, *Highway Program Shows Limited Progress Toward Increasing Accessibility To and Through Appalachia*, B-164497(3), May 12, 1971, pp. 8, 22.

11. *1973 Annual Report of the Appalachian Regional Commission*, p. 19.

12. U.S. General Accounting Office, *Highway Program Shows Limited Progress*, pp. 28-29.

13. Appalachian Regional Commission, "Education Goals and Strategies, A Preliminary Report of the Education Subcommittee to The Appalachian Regional Commission," August 1974 (unpublished draft) (mimeo.), p. 14.

14. "Critical Health Manpower Shortage Areas, Designations and Withdrawals," *The Federal Register*, February 25, 1975, Part II, pp. 8156-8161.

15. Appalachian Regional Commission, *1974 Annual Report of the Appalachian Regional Commission*, pp. 53-54.

16. Appalachian Regional Commission, *The Appalachian Experiment 1965-1970*, pp. 49-50.

17. U.S. Congress, Senate, *Regional Development Act of 1975*, Report of the Committee on Public Works, July 14, 1975 (Washington: Government Printing Office, 1975), p. 42.

18. "The New Appalachian Subregions and Their Development Strategies," *Appalachia*, August-September 1974, pp. 11-22.

Chapter 6
Public Works: Foundations
for Growth

1. U.S. Office of Management and Budget, *Special Analysis Budget of the United States Government, Fiscal Year 1974* (Washington: Government Printing Office, 1973), p. 226.

2. Center for Political Research, *Economic Activities Affecting Location of Economic Development*, final report prepared for the Economic Development Administration, U.S. Department of Commerce, November 1970.

3. David K. Harley, Janet W. Patton, and Lucia B. Findley, "The Regional Impacts of Federal Policy," in U.S. Congress, House, *A National Public Works Investment Policy*, background papers prepared for the Committee on Public Works (Washington: Government Printing Office, November 1974), pp. 92-93.

4. U.S. Congress, House, *Evaluation of Economic Development Programs—Part II*, Hearings before the Special Subcommittee on Economic Development Programs of the Committee on Public Works, 91st Cong., 2d Sess. (Washington: Government Printing Office, September 10, 20, and 21, 1970), pp. 17-24.

5. U.S. Department of Commerce, Economic Development Administration, Office of Administration and Program Analysis, *A Comparative Analysis of the Impacts Resulting from 50 Public Works Projects, 1970, 1974*, December 1974 (mimeo.), p. 2.

6. EBS Management Consultants, Inc., *A Methodology for Evaluation of the Economic Development Administration's Public Works Programs*, prepared for U.S. Department of Commerce, Economic Development Administration, May 1969 (mimeo.).

7. EBS Management Consultants, Inc., *A Pilot Evaluation of Twenty-Four EDA Public Works Projects*, prepared for U.S. Department of Commerce, Economic Development Administration, November 1969; Boise Cascade Center for Community Development, *An Evaluation of EDA Public Works Projects*, prepared for the U.S. Department of Commerce, Economic Development Administration, September 1970 (mimeo.), (2 vols.); and U.S. Department of Commerce, Economic Development Administration, *The Economic Development Administration's Public Works Program: An Evaluation* (Washington: U.S. Department of Commerce, July 1970).

8. Centaur Management Consultants, Inc., *Re-Evaluation of the Impacts of Fifty Public Works Projects*, prepared for U.S. Department of Commerce, Economic Development Administration, November 1974 (mimeo.).

9. U.S. Department of Commerce, Economic Development Administration, Office of Administration and Program Analysis, *An Updated Evaluation of EDA-Funded Industrial Parks, 1968-1974*, June 1974 (mimeo.), pp. 6-8.

10. Ibid.

11. U.S. Department of Commerce, *1974 Annual Report, Economic Development Administration* (Washington: Government Printing Office, 1975), p. 17.

12. Development Associates, Inc., *An Evaluation of EDA Training Related Projects, Findings-Analysis-Conclusion-Recommendations*, prepared for the U.S. Department of Commerce, Economic Development Administration, 1972, p. iv-3.

13. U.S. Department of Commerce, Economic Development Administration, Office of Administration and Program Analysis, *Evaluation of the Oregon Shakespearean Festival Expansion*, April 1972 (mimeo.).

14. Centaur Management Consultants, Inc., *Evaluation of Impact of Tourism/Recreation Projects for Economic Development Administration*, Vol. I, Evaluation Results and Methodology, prepared for

U.S. Department of Commerce, Economic Development Administration, June 1973 (mimeo.), p. xi.

15. Ibid., *Appendix D*, pp. D-190 to D-202.

16. U.S. Department of Commerce, Economic Development Administration, *EDA in Oakland: A 1974 Update*, July 1974 (mimeo.), pp. 12-14.

17. Jeffrey L. Pressman and Aaron B. Wildavsky, *Implementation: How Great Expectations in Washington are Dashed in Oakland* (Berkeley: University of California Press, 1973), Chap. 3.

18. U.S. Department of Commerce, *EDA in Oakland*, pp. 1-2.

19. Boise Cascade Center for Community Development, *Indian Economic Development, An Evaluation of EDA's Selected Indian Reservation Program*, Vol. I, prepared for U.S. Department of Commerce, Economic Development Administration, July 1972 (mimeo.), p. 51.

20. Centaur Management Consultants, Inc., *Evaluation of Impact of Tourism/Recreation Projects*, pp. D-301–D-312.

21. U.S. Department of Commerce, Economic Development Administration, *An Updated Evaluation of EDA-Funded Industrial Parks, 1968-1974*, pp. 46-51.

22. Boise Cascade Center for Economic Development, *Indian Economic Development*, pp. 39-41.

23. U.S. Department of Commerce, Economic Development Administration, *An Updated Evaluation of EDA-Funded Industrial Parks 1968-1974*, p. 46.

24. U.S. Department of Commerce, Economic Development Administration, Office of Administration and Program Analysis, *Analysis of the Costs of EDA's Public Works Program*, September 1971 (mimeo.), p. 24.

25. Boise Cascade Center for Community Development, *An Evaluation of Public Works Projects, Volume I*, p. 38; and U.S. Department of Commerce, Economic Development Administration, *A Comparative Analysis of the Impacts Resulting from 50 Public Works Projects, 1970, 1974*, pp. iv-v.

26. Boise Cascade Center for Community Development, *An Evaluation of EDA Public Works Projects, Vol. 1*, p. 36.

27. Centaur Management Consultants, Inc., *Re-Evaluation of the Impacts of Fifty Public Works Projects.*

28. U.S. Department of Commerce, Economic Development Ad-

ministration, *An Updated Evaluation of EDA-Funded Industrial Parks, 1968-1974.*

29. U.S. Department of Commerce, Economic Development Administration, *A Comparative Analysis of the Impacts Resulting from 50 Public Works Projects, 1970, 1974*, p. 41.

30. U.S. Department of Commerce, Economic Development Administration, *An Updated Evaluation of EDA-Funded Industrial Parks, 1968-1974*, p. 12.

31. Ibid.

32. U.S. Congress, Senate, *Accelerated Public Works In Retrospect and Prospect*, a staff report to the Committee on Public Works, 88th Cong., 1st Sess. (Washington: Government Printing Office, December 1963), p. 20; and U.S. Department of Commerce, Economic Development Administration, *An Evaluation of the Public Works Impact Program(PWIP)*, Final Report, January 1975, p. 11 (mimeo.).

33. Sar A. Levitan, *Federal Aid to Depressed Areas*, Table 5-5, p. 158; and U.S. Congress, Senate, *Accelerated Public Works in Retrospect and Prospect*, Table III, p. 14.

34. U.S. General Accounting Office, *Overstatement of Number of Jobs Created Under the Accelerated Public Works Program*, Washington, D.C., May 1964.

35. U.S. Department of Commerce, *An Evaluation of the Public Works Impact Program (PWIP)*, Table II.C.1, p. 33.

36. Nancy H. Teeters, "The 1972 Budget: Where it Stands and Where it Might Go," *Brookings Papers on Economic Activity 1:1971* (Washington: The Brookings Institution, 1971), p. 233.

Chapter 7
Business Development

1. U.S. Department of Commerce, *Economic Development Administration, The EDA Experience in the Evolution of Policy, A Brief History September 1965-June 1973*, May 1974 (mimeo.), p. 15.

2. U.S. Department of Commerce, *1975 Annual Report, Economic Development Administration*, in press.

3. U.S. Department of Commerce, Economic Development Administration, *Management Summary Report as of December 31, 1974*, pt. 4.

4. Stanley Miller, Darius Gaskins and Charles Liner, *Evaluation of the ARA-EDA Loan Program*, Office of Economic Research, Economic Development Administration, November 10, 1968 (mimeo.), pp. 7-23.

5. Chilton Research Services and CONSAD Research Corporation, *An Evaluation of the Economic Development Administration's Business Loan Program*, prepared for U.S. Department of Commerce, Economic Development Administration, July 1969 (mimeo.), pp. 6.12 to 6.28.

6. Booz, Allen and Hamilton, Inc., *An Evaluation of the Business Loan Program of the Economic Development Administration, Part I: A National Assessment*, prepared for U.S. Department of Commerce, Economic Development Administration, July 1970 (mimeo.), p. 22.

7. Chilton Research Services and CONSAD Research Corporation, *An Evaluation of the Economic Development Administration's Business Loan Program*, p. 3.5.

8. Booz, Allen and Hamilton, Inc., *An Evaluation of the Business Loan Program of the Economic Development Administration, Part I*, p. 13.

9. Chilton Research Services, *Multiple Job Shifts Associated with EDA Business Loans*, prepared for U.S. Department of Commerce, Economic Development Administration, June 1970 (mimeo.), p. 5.

10. U.S. Department of Agriculture, Rural Development Service, *Rural Development, Fifth Annual Report of the President to the Congress on Governmental Services to Rural America* (Washington: Government Printing Office, 1975), p. 52.

11. "USDA Delivers Credit for Rural Development," *U.S. Department of Agriculture News*, August 2, 1974.

12. *From the State Capitals* (Asbury Park, N.J.: Bethune Jones), July 1, 1975 and August 1, 1975.

Chapter 8
The Uncertain Balance Sheet

1. U.S. Department of Commerce, Economic Development Administration, Growth Center Evaluation Task Force, *Program Evaluation: The Economic Development Administration Growth Center Strategy*, February 1972 (mimeo.), pp. 13-20; and David F. Darwent, *An Analysis of Recent Survey Data on the Economic Development*

Administration's Growth Center Policy, prepared for the U.S. Department of Commerce, Economic Development Administration, May 1973 (mimeo.), pp. 19-21.

List of Figures

List of Tables

List of Maps

Index

Index

About the Authors

Sar A. Levitan (Ph.D., Columbia University) is Research Professor of Economics and Director of the Center for Social Policy Studies at The George Washington University. The Center is funded by a grant from The Ford Foundation. Dr. Levitan has been a consultant to various governmental agencies and has served on labor panels for the Federal Mediation and Conciliation Service and the American Arbitration Association. Included among his many books are *The Promise of Greatness* (with Robert Taggart), *Programs in Aid of the Poor for the 1970s*, Third Edition, and *Federal Aid to Depressed Areas*.

Joyce K. Zickler, a candidate for the Ph.D. in Economics at The George Washington University, is an economist with the Federal Reserve Board. She is the coauthor (with Sar A. Levitan) of *The Quest for a Federal Manpower Partnership*.